LIBERTY

T0316240

Glyn Maxwell

LIBERTY

'If the world's so very young, it'll scream until it's fed…'

OBERON BOOKS
LONDON

First published in 2008 by Oberon Books Ltd
521 Caledonian Road, London N7 9RH

Copyright © Glyn Maxwell, 2008

Glyn Maxwell is hereby identified as author of this play
in accordance with section 77 of the Copyright, Designs and
Patents Act 1988. The author has asserted his moral rights.

All rights whatsoever in this play are strictly reserved and
application for performance etc. should be made before
commencement of rehearsal to Micheline Steinberg Associates,
104 Great Portland Street, London W1W 6PE
(info@steinplays.com). No performance may be given unless a
licence has been obtained, and no alterations may be made in
the title or the text of the play without the author's prior written
consent.

You may not copy, store, distribute, transmit, reproduce or
otherwise make available this publication (or any part of it) in
any form, or binding or by any means (print, electronic, digital,
optical, mechanical, photocopying, recording or otherwise),
without the prior written permission of the publisher. Any person
who does any unauthorized act in relation to this publication may
be liable to criminal prosecution and civil claims for damages.

A catalogue record for this book is available from the British
Library.

PB ISBN: 9781840028690
E ISBN: 9781786820013

Cover design by Feast Design

Persons in the Play

EVARISTE GAMELIN
a struggling artist, later a Revolutionary Magistrate

PHILIPPE DEMAY
a supplier of food to the Revolutionary Army

MAURICE BROTTEAUX
formerly the Duke of Ilettes, now a puppet-maker

ELODIE BLAISE
an embroidress

ROSE CLEBERT
a comedienne at the National Theatre

LOUISE ROCHEMAURE
formerly a socialite, now a businesswoman

Magistrates at the Tribunals:
TRUBERT   RENAUDIN
DUPONT   BEAUVISAGE

The Section Police:
NAVETTE   BELLIER
GUENOT   DELOURMEL

The Prison Guards:
CHALIER   JAVOGUES
LACROIX

SANSCULOTTES

SETTING

The play begins outside Paris in May 1793 (Prairial, Year 1). France is ruled by the Committee of Public Safety, whose most important figure is Maximilien Robespierre. Louis XVI was executed in January; Marie-Antoinette is in prison. Revolutionary France has declared war on all its neighbours.

Liberty was first performed in August 2008 at Shakespeare's Globe Theatre, with the following cast:

EVARISTE GAMELIN, David Sturzaker

ELODIE BLAISE, Ellie Piercy

PHILIPPE DEMAY, Edward Macliam

ROSE CLEBERT, Kirsty Besterman

LOUISE ROCHEMAURE, Belinda Lang

MAURICE BROTTEAUX, John Bett

TRUBERT, DUPONT, BELLIER, GUENOT, LACROIX, JAVOGUES, Gregory Gudgeon

RENAUDIN, BEAUVISAGE, NAVETTE, DELOURMEL, CHALIER, Jonty Stephens

Director Guy Retallack
Designer Ti Green
Composer William Lyons
Choreographer Paul Harris

Liberty was commissioned by Sue Scott Davison for Lifeblood Theatre Company and produced in association with Shakespeare's Globe Theatre.

ACT ONE

DAY VII, MONTH OF MEADOWS, YEAR I

SANSCULOTTES   Brothers, sisters, the sun is rising
Darkness flees and the world is white
Tyrants swing from the branches bending
Princes pale in the morning light
   Sing, Citizens
   O sing, Freedom
The page is turning and it shines so bright!

Sunlight crosses every stream and meadow
Sunlight enters every house and tower
Sharp as steel it will find each shadow
Cut them down where they cringe and cower
   Sing, Citizens
   O sing, Freedom
Now begins your everlasting hour!

Blue is the sky for the hour is glorious
White are the hearts of the virtuous poor
Red are the rags of the rich man helpless
France is free and for ever more
   Sing, Citizens
   O sing, Freedom
Fly your tricolours and march to war!

EVARISTE alone, on a Picnic Day

EVARISTE   Men are...
Men are born and remain...
Men are born and remain...free...and equal...
Men are born and remain free and equal!
Can you hear, that, Citizens, can you remember
what we – no...when we – no...
Can you hear that, Citizens, can you hear that echo
out through space and time? All of the earth
can hear us, the future can – no...We are at war,

7

my friends, we are…no no…
Long live France! – no no that's at the end…
We are at war, my friends,
for freedom, for equality, and yet…
we live while others – no –
we feast while others – what –
we feast while others starve, we are at war!
War with the ones who – no...
The world is at war with us, on the battlefield,
in the mind, in the very halls of the Assembly,
and here we are, alone…
one Nation, one People, the first ones…
and here we stand, alone…

ELODIE applauds

ELODIE   You're not alone,
               Monsieur Gamelin, you only think you are.

EVARISTE   I did – I'm sorry – I thought –

ELODIE   You found a space,
               you found a natural audience in the meadows!
               You're an orator, Monsieur Gamelin, or you are
               when no one's looking.

EVARISTE   I'm just – you were very quiet.
               How did you find me?

ELODIE   Easy!
               This is the highest place for miles. Of course
               you came here, you can see the world!

EVARISTE   I came here
               to be alone.

ELODIE   You failed!
               Philippe told everyone in the whole picnic
               to meet here in an hour – he won't say why!
               To listen to you, do you think? Are you practising
               your picnic speech?

EVARISTE   I – no –

ELODIE   You know it off by heart, are you an actor?
Philippe says you're an artist, but I thought
he meant with paint.

EVARISTE   I am, I was, with paint,
indeed, when we were students, as you say.

ELODIE   But now you're a Patriot first.

EVARISTE   I am. Of course!

ELODIE   But everyone says they are, you may as well
announce you have two eyes. I'm more excited
by someone being an artist! Now on this picnic
we have *two* artists, you and Philippe; that actress,
and she's a kind of artist, an *artiste*!
and that old man, I don't know what he does,
and Mme Louise, she knows important people;
then me, I don't do much!

EVARISTE   You play your part
I'm sure.

ELODIE   I play my part in the Revolution!
Where would we be without embroidery?
We'd be overrun by tyrants! That was my joke,
Monsieur Gamelin, you don't have to look so
  shocked.
You can chuckle if you like, it is a picnic.
We're not in Paris now.

EVARISTE   I realize
we're not in Paris. I'm not sure where we are…
I do know we're at war with all the world's
tyrannies, and if we lose that war
we'll be wiped from history.

ELODIE   Well. It's nice to chat.

EVARISTE   I – look, I'm sorry –
you caught me in –

9

ELODIE   I caught you in full cry!

EVARISTE   Well as you say, I mean, I'm full of thoughts
                I need to say aloud, does that make sense?

ELODIE   It does, it's just like me, I have thoughts too,
                but then I'm already speaking when I have them,
                or I have them the next week. And today's Sunday,
                Monsieur Gamelin, so I shan't have any!
                Except to say it's not called Sunday now,
                it's Picnic Day, see *I* can make new laws.
                It's our day away from everything, it's Philippe's
                grand idea! And he wanted you to meet me.

EVARISTE   And so I did, at the great fat feast of plenty.
                I met you, I'm enchanted.

ELODIE   Picnic Day,
                in the Month of Flowers!

EVARISTE   *Prairial*, Month of Meadows.

ELODIE   Meadows, Flowers, it all smells as sweet
                on a holiday.

EVARISTE   If one requires a holiday
                from history.

ELODIE   *You* do. Look at you,
                all pale. And I'm still calling it May
                myself, that's warm with memories, don't you think,
                it's colourful! The new word, how'd you say it?

EVARISTE   *Prairial.*

ELODIE   It sounds as pale as you are.

EVARISTE   I'm naturally pale, Mademoiselle Blaise.

ELODIE   How naturally interesting! And *Blaise*,
                that's only my daddy's name, the old regime,
                I swept it away in a blaze of Elodie!

EVARISTE   Elodie.

ELODIE
Yes and you're Evariste Gamelin,
who's naturally pale.

EVARISTE
And tired, and hungry.

ELODIE
'Course you are, you're naturally hungry!
There's us all having a picnic by the stream
and you just march right off, don't you remember?
Was it my company?

EVARISTE
No no of course not,
It was – company, it was I don't know, I'm sorry,
there were words that needed saying –

ELODIE
Elodie...

EVARISTE
Elodie.

ELODIE
That needed saying!

EVARISTE
It did...
Elodie.

ELODIE
You've forgotten where you were!
You were at war!

EVARISTE
I was, we are, of course,
so I put my mind to a speech, about the war –
because...we set a picnic on a blanket,
as if there *is* no war but there *is* a war,
our brothers fighting, dying for our beliefs –

ELODIE
*The world is at war with us, on the battlefield,
in the mind, in the very halls of the Assembly,
and here we are, alone.*

EVARISTE
Did I say that?

ELODIE
You did! And now *I* have! I'm like a parrot,
my daddy always says, I hear things once
and don't forget them. Don't know what they mean,
but I can cry them out from my little cage!
Feed me on nuts and seeds and I'm more than happy.

I should have been good at school but I stayed home.
Who was it for?

EVARISTE   For?

ELODIE   Who's your speech for?

EVARISTE   For – the People.

ELODIE   What people? The Tree People!
They're very quiet, Monsieur Evariste Gamelin.

EVARISTE   They are, they're deep in thought,
though when the wind gets up they start applauding.

ELODIE   *I* think they're thinking that it's four years now,
four years of liberty, equality,
speeches, songs and anthems, four years
marching on palaces and heads on pikes,
men hanging from the branches or the lampposts
and massacres and ghastliness, *I* think
they're thinking what I'm thinking – can we not
take one day of rest? I mean the Lord did.
Am I meant to say 'the Lord'?

EVARISTE   You are free, Elodie,
to do as you please. Four years ago you were not.

ELODIE   Oh I know, I only think we maybe earned
a holiday, don't you? You don't at all.
I'm surrounded by your followers!

EVARISTE   You are.
These trees can hear you, Elodie. You can see them
swaying, that's them thinking.

ELODIE   Trees, trees,
you are free, trees, to stand where you want to stand,
to stroll about, to dance! Oaks and poplars,
shrubs and hedges, hand in hand, rise up,
march on the town!

EVARISTE   It's true,
you're joking but it's true!

ELODIE   May I go on joking
whether or not it's true?

EVARISTE   You see at the birth
of all of this was a man who found in Nature
what Man had lost.

ELODIE   At the end of this is a girl
trying to say hello to you!

EVARISTE   I'm – sorry –

ELODIE   You're sorry, bit late for that, here comes the
       Committee
of Public Safety!

PHILIPPE, ROSE

PHILIPPE   Guilty as charged, in the flesh!
Now this man's face is white on a summer's day:
aristocrat!

ELODIE   He's not going to laugh, Philippe,
I tried that, it was hopeless. When I found him –
no that's our little secret…

PHILIPPE   Genius,
you and this girl have grown a little secret?
Now that's quick work. Hey Clebert, don't you think,
can we not work that quickly?

ROSE   In your dreams
I'm sure we do, Philippe, but that's not me,
I send my understudy.

PHILIPPE   She does nicely,
Clebert, can I keep her?

ROSE   If you pay her.

ELODIE   Rose, can I call you Rose, I'll give away
nothing about the secret but a clue is:
you may not be the only star performer
hereabouts!

EVARISTE   The First Law of Picnics:
you go in search of solitude, you find
everyone.

PHILIPPE   That's Genius in a nutshell.
Finds the loneliest spot and the loveliest view
and thinks it belongs to him.

EVARISTE   I made the mistake
of thinking I was free, on – Picnic Day.

ELODIE   That's what it's called, Philippe, we changed its name!

PHILIPPE   So you like my little friend the embroidress?

EVARISTE   Ah, you're a friend of *his*, well then I blink
and you're gone on the merry-go-round.

ELODIE   But I come back
waving, don't I, Evariste?

PHILIPPE   First names,
I see.

ELODIE   Now I'm a friend of *Evariste's*,
and [*PHILIPPE*] who are you? I've forgotten…

PHILIPPE   I sell tickets
for the merry-go-round and this boy owes me money.

PHILIPPE draws EVARISTE aside

PHILIPPE   Where did you disappear to?

EVARISTE   Thin air.
Clear air. Air that's pure. And don't call me
Genius.

PHILIPPE   Or what'll the Genius do?

EVARISTE   I'll call you Prodigy.

PHILIPPE   But I don't mind that,
           plus it's true, I *am* a Prodigy,
           I'm just getting on a bit, I'll get round to it,
           that masterpiece up my sleeve, but in the mean time,
           Genius, she can't take her eyes off you.

EVARISTE   When the Revolution's over I'll wave.

PHILIPPE   Yes you can stroke what's left of her white hair.
           'When the Revolution's over…'

EVARISTE   I don't need
           to forget, Philippe, I don't need a day off
           anything.

PHILIPPE   You need to eat, Genius,
           not nibble at your lettuce like some rabbit
           when everybody's eating what they want to
           for the first time in weeks. You made them all feel
           guilty.

EVARISTE   So they were guilty. I wasn't hungry.

PHILIPPE   Of course you're fucking hungry, we're all hungry.
           You think it's easy setting up a banquet
           in the ruins of this shit?

EVARISTE   No I don't think
           it's easy at all, Philippe.

PHILIPPE   It's Prodigy.

EVARISTE   Prodigy.

PHILIPPE   It's the devil to get this stuff.
           You wouldn't believe.

EVARISTE   Good. I don't want to know.

PHILIPPE   Of course you don't. No one with principles
           ever wants to know. I got rid of mine
           and the world turned fascinating.

EVARISTE   The world?
It turned its face towards the light, Philippe,
and we were there at sunrise.

PHILIPPE   Oh I say,
very poetic.

EVARISTE   I mean it, and you mean it,
don't pretend, we were alive to breathe it –
liberty, equality – do you not
wake up and think you dreamed it?

PHILIPPE   No the things
I dream aren't possible or in fact legal.
I joke. You smile.

EVARISTE   There's not a single line
you won't bend into a grin. Not one straight road
in your country, just diversions.

PHILIPPE   And bistros,
excellent little bistros. Oh I'm with you,
Evariste, your new world –

EVARISTE   *Our* new world –

PHILIPPE   *Our* new world of course, Christ of course,
sunrise, sunlight, sunshine,
I'm as proud a Patriot as you, it's only –
when did your sense of humour mount the scaffold,
and what were its last words?

EVARISTE   Oh it's in exile.
In London. If it comes back, arrest it.

PHILIPPE   Can I steal its jokes?

EVARISTE   You already stole its jokes,
you frisked it at the border.

PHILIPPE   Guilty as charged. Evariste,
don't go away, don't – *half* of you go away!
What can I do with half a Genius?

EVARISTE   You?
                Flog it to the other half.

PHILIPPE   I mean it!
                The nuts are taking over.
                We're all going to need a sodding sense of humour.

ELODIE, ROSE

ELODIE   Stop being serious *now*! It's Picnic Day,
                isn't it, Sister Rose?
                Rose and me are sisters, not just sisters
                in the Revolution, sisters in the heart.

ROSE   Sisters in the afternoon.

ELODIE   And for always.

PHILIPPE   Can I be a sister too? I was once a brother
                for him, we were the stars of our school year,
                but Genius, he's a creature of the future
                when nobody needs to eat.

ELODIE   Are you really,
                Evariste, a creature of the future?

PHILIPPE   I'm going to escort you, Elodie, to safety,
                before I lose you too, and, in her stead,
                Genius, I leave you yet another
                pearl of my acquaintance. What a union!
                The undiscovered genius of the canvas,
                and the famous –

ROSE   Chorus girl.

PHILIPPE   She is so modest.
                Modest Clebert.

PHILIPPE and ELODIE go

ROSE   I'm sure Monsieur Gamelin
                has work to do in some cornfield.

EVARISTE   Not at all,
             it's Picnic Day. Hooray. Shall we do handstands?

ROSE   Do what you like, express yourself, fly a kite,
             I've lines to learn, I've twelve whole lines to learn.

EVARISTE   *Pamela...*

ROSE   *Pamela*, yep. Do you know it?

EVARISTE   I know of its content.

ROSE   Right. So you don't know it.
             Everyone knows of its content.

EVARISTE   Everyone knows
             it's meant to inspire nostalgia for a world
             we've left behind.

ROSE   You mean it's got dukes in it.

EVARISTE takes the book

             What, are you going to burn it?

EVARISTE   Why would I burn it?
             You need it. 'The poor Fellow's ready to cry: I have
               been telling him that he has done his part to my
               Ruin, so his Repentance does me no good.'

ROSE   'I'll assure you, Madam, I should be as ready to cry as
               he, if I should do you any Harm.'

EVARISTE   'It is not in his Power to help it now, but your part
               is to come, and you may choose whether you'll
               contribute to my Ruin or not.'

ROSE   'Why look ye, look ye, Madam, I...' Wait. I know it.
               No.

EVARISTE   'Great notion.'

ROSE   What? Oh yes!
             'Why look ye, look ye, Madam, I have a great notion
               of doing my duty to my Master.'

EVARISTE   Very good. Parrot fashion.

EVARISTE gives it back

ROSE   Was that a review?
                Why thank you sir. You on the other hand
                were perfectly rotten. She's a ruined woman,
                you should get out and meet some.

EVARISTE   I could just
                come to your theatre, couldn't I.

ROSE   Oh you're witty.

EVARISTE   'My duty to my Master…' How can you speak this?
                It's nothing to do with anything.

ROSE   Yes, it's to do with
                Rose being able to eat. Now I have to practise.

EVARISTE   Sister Rose –

ROSE   Could you not call me that.

EVARISTE   A play about the English landed gentry
                at a time when France is fighting for its life
                against this very tyr/anny –

ROSE   /Philippe and I
                were playing this game at lunch, I think you lose
                a point for talking politics, five points
                for mentioning the war. You've lost so many
                the flowers are dying.

EVARISTE   Ah, but I don't lose points
                if I don't observe the game.

ROSE   Ah, very true,
                the voice of the Committee, very true.

EVARISTE   Ah, nothing's *very* true. It's either true
                or false. It's right or wrong. It's good or evil.

ROSE   What's that, a philosophy?

EVARISTE   It's not a play.
            We have deposed a king.

ROSE   Oh and he's ten points,
            I forgot to say.

EVARISTE   Laid waste a tyranny.

ROSE   I'm a Parisienne, Monsieur Gamelin,
            I don't need to be told there've been some changes.

EVARISTE   Yes, *every* man has value.

ROSE   Meanwhile, women?

EVARISTE   Every citizen, woman, child, has value.

ROSE   I believed that anyway. That's why
            I took a stick and marched off to Versailles
            in '89 – were you there? didn't see you –
            because I believed in justice.

EVARISTE   We can all
            believe in what we want, yet there was never
            a Nation that enshrined equality
            as a principle.

ROSE   America.

EVARISTE   A new world
            in a wilderness. But we have made the old world
            young again.

ROSE   If the world's so very young
            it'll scream until it's fed.

EVARISTE   Aren't you glad?
            Do you regret what's gone? Is that the reason
            you dress up every night and say twelve lines
            no one will ever say again?

ROSE   I'm glad,
            Evariste, 'Citizen', that I'm alive,
            and I love what work I have. It's all I'd wish

on anyone. Now I wish to learn these lines
no one will ever say, so I can say them.

PHILIPPE, ELODIE

PHILIPPE   Evariste, what have you done to this girl?
            You are her only subject.

ELODIE   Sister Rose,
            did you get this man to smile at all?

ROSE   There is smiling
            or weeping. There is salt or there is pepper.

EVARISTE   I was strolling in the old world, with a duchess.

ROSE   And I was on the moon, with a philosopher.

ELODIE   She's an actress, not a duchess,
            we don't have duchesses! I'm taking him away
            from your bad influence, Philippe.

PHILIPPE   Oh take him,
            he's hungry, feed him butterflies.

PHILIPPE and ROSE one way, EVARISTE and ELODIE another

ELODIE   She's an actress, Evariste dear, she's famous!
            Or not quite famous but she's at the National.
            She used to play princesses.

EVARISTE   Princesses.
            A theatre calling itself the National
            should be at the disposal of the Nation,
            some might say, not playing at princesses.

ELODIE   *Disposal, the Nation, some might say –*
            You're talking to me now!
            Rose is my sister in the Revolution.
            She marched in '89 but then she's older.
            I *would* have marched! We'd have been side by side,
            me and you, in a crowd, we'd have got talking,
            don't you think? Wielding two sharp pikes
            but also chatting. What would you have said?

21

EVARISTE   Nothing, I'd have been shy.

ELODIE   Are you still shy?
            I'm glad we didn't meet then, for we've met now.
            How come you don't know Rose if you know
               Philippe?

EVARISTE   He's my best friend. I'm one of his ten thousand.

ELODIE   I'm one of them as well. I'm *number* ten thousand!

EVARISTE   We go our ways. We have what we always had,
            we are what we always were.

ELODIE   What about those two?

MAURICE and LOUISE in the distance

EVARISTE   Oh no they're coming our way.

ELODIE   Do you not like them?
            I thought they were friends of yours.

EVARISTE   No, they are…

ELODIE   I've never met them before –

EVARISTE   No they are my friends –
            but I want to be with you.
            I mean only you. I can't
            quite believe I said that.

ELODIE   Neither can I!
            Do you want to say it again, see if you did do?

EVARISTE   You can tell me, can't you, parrot?

ELODIE   You did say it.
            Then *I* said let's run away, or I'm about to.
            It's like – being in the future, being together!

*EVARISTE and ELODIE run off. LOUISE ahead, MAURICE behind, with
everything*

LOUISE   Where did he go? If I didn't have to wait
                for you, Maurice, we'd have found him. That's the
                  thing,
                it's you, they are young people, it's your stories
                at lunch, too many stories.

MAURICE   I'm not sure
                I spoke two minutes in two hours, Louise.

LOUISE   It was an unjust world, the world you lived in,
                it makes them feel uncomfortable.

MAURICE   Which is why
                I only speak if spoken to.

LOUISE   Evariste
                has clearly asked Philippe to invite me
                because of my connections.

MAURICE   Your connections.

LOUISE   Evariste has friends in high places.
                I too am well connected. I can make
                that boy a proposition.

MAURICE   A younger lady
                was doing that at lunch.

LOUISE   Oh nonsense,
                the embroidress? She's a dimwit,
                and he's going to be something big.

MAURICE   Yes I don't doubt it.
                I live in his house, Louise, you can make connections
                any time, but you never visit. Is it
                my past life as a symbol of oppression?

LOUISE   Don't be absurd. It's just not a part of town
                one visits. Now come on, we have to find him!

LOUISE goes, MAURICE follows

PHILIPPE and ROSE emerge

23

PHILIPPE   That was close.

ROSE   *Is* that why you asked Louise?
             So she could meet Evariste?

PHILIPPE   She asked herself,
             and was delighted to accept. The old chap's
             come along to keep her company
             so we don't have to. How did you like Evariste
             the starving artist?

ROSE   He doesn't much like actors.
             He made me feel I'd been interrogated.

PHILIPPE   That's just old Genius, he can see the lines
             of his ideals inscribed on the actual air,
             like a blueprint. If you're there,
             he drew you. If you're not, well he can't see you.

ROSE   I felt – I was suddenly proud of what I do.
             I haven't been that for years.

PHILIPPE   Proud Clebert.

ROSE   Are you all right, Philippe?

PHILIPPE   Oh seventh heaven.
             Well third or fourth. Why wouldn't I be all right?

ROSE   Because you love her.

PHILIPPE   Do I? Who?

ROSE   Philippe…
             Elodie.

PHILIPPE   I never said I loved her.

ROSE   You did six months ago.

PHILIPPE   Six months ago
             the king still had a head. Six months ago
             we'd never heard of Monsieur Robespierre
             the Incorruptible. And Public Safety

was trying not to put your foot in horseshit.
Now it's nine lunatics in charge of France.

ROSE   You've lost about eighty points.

PHILIPPE   Of course I love her,
everyone loves her. Anyway I love you.

ROSE   Talking of horseshit.

PHILIPPE   Why won't Evariste eat?

ROSE   Well, in so much as I care, I'd say it's because
morally he thinks he should be hungry.
Admirable, in an irritating fashion.

PHILIPPE   Now there's a character sketch: Evariste
caught in two words… We used to do that at school,
sketches, take a charcoal, five minutes,
capture the other's soul.

ROSE   What did you draw,
a stick-man.

PHILIPPE   I don't know, I can't remember.
I always said his was better. So did he.

ROSE   He's probably wondering where you got this food
    from.
Is it your army work?

PHILIPPE   They have to eat,
soldiers, you know, like pigs.

ROSE   And you're the farmer.
Be careful, won't you. The Committee don't like
    money.

PHILIPPE   They like it when it's trodden into wine.
And you've not had enough. We need wine,
and we need to start the game.

ROSE   We do? What game.

PHILIPPE   My game.

ROSE   Don't like the sound of that. What's *he* called?

PHILIPPE   What's who called.

ROSE   The old boy with Louise,
we didn't speak at lunch.

PHILIPPE   Only Louise
spoke at lunch, it's traditional.

ROSE   They're lost,
they're going round in circles.

PHILIPPE   Keep your head down,
they'll see us!

ROSE   You're ridiculous. Look,
she's made him carry everything, he must be
ancient, go and help him.

PHILIPPE   That's Maurice,
Maurice Brotteaux. You know who he used to be?
The Duke of Ilettes.

ROSE   No, of the wild parties?
Isn't he dead?

PHILIPPE   Does he look dead?

ROSE   Well sort of,
but only because he's listening to Louise.

PHILIPPE   No, in his head he's talking with Lucretius
on the pointlessness of life. I suppose life
does have a little more point when you own a castle.

ROSE   The Duke of Ilettes…does Monsieur Genius know
he's on a picnic with a duke?

PHILIPPE   Of course,
he's Evariste's old friend.

ROSE   You're such a liar.

PHILIPPE	Didn't you hear him say? He lives in Evariste's attic. He's the lodger. I'm serious.
ROSE	Yes. You're a serious liar.
PHILIPPE	Evariste's mother was a chambermaid in his old chateau. Course he lost the lot in '89 and she hid him in the attic. But to her he was still the master: she would curtsy as he climbed down the ladder. Evariste would scold her: 'Mother, you mustn't do that! Don't you know you're as good as he is?' The old girl died at Christmas, trying to remember the new name for Christmas.
ROSE	Gamelin has a duke for a friend, how funny.
PHILIPPE	In the attic, living proof a duke can embrace his poverty and starve with the best of them. He carries his Lucretius everywhere, it's pretty much all he has.
ROSE	So a former aristocrat *and* an atheist. I think I'd live in an attic on the moon.
PHILIPPE	The Committee's still deciding about God, though. He's at the door, it could go either way. And they don't mind godlessness in the dirt poor, just in the ones who had it all. Ungrateful, you see, that's decadence.
ROSE	But Gamelin is kind to him?
PHILIPPE	He's an old man. Evariste is kind to the kind of people people are kind to. Now she's seen us.
ROSE	How does he know Louise?

27

PHILIPPE   Everyone knows Louise.
                   She was there in the good old bad old days.

ROSE   *Monsignor
                   le Duc des Ilettes.* Those old bags at the National
                   drone on about his parties. How they'll hate me
                   if I get to know him.

PHILIPPE   What are you waiting for?

LOUISE, MAURICE with his book, and all the bags

ROSE   Sit, sir, we should have helped you –

MAURICE   We saw you,
                   we saw you from afar, you drew us on,
                   it was all the help we needed.

LOUISE   [*PHILIPPE*] *You'll* need help
                   monsieur, when I've had my say!

PHILIPPE   When will that be,
                   November?

LOUISE   What, 'November'? You mean *Brumaire*,
                   the Month of Fog.

ROSE   Oh jolly good, you've learned them.

PHILIPPE slips away

LOUISE   Have you not, Sister Rose?

ROSE   I don't even know
                   what day it is.

LOUISE   Today is the seventh day
                   of *Prairial*, or the Month of Meadows. The Year:
                   Year One.

ROSE   Yes, for babies.

LOUISE   Silly woman.

ROSE   What if one morning in the Month of Fog…

LOUISE	*Brumaire.*
ROSE	…You wake up and it isn't foggy? Does someone get arrested?
LOUISE	Yes. You do. I was talking about Monsieur Evariste Gamelin. Philippe – where is Philippe?
ROSE	He's gone to fetch a game we have to play, it's the Hour of Games, it used to be called sunset.
LOUISE	Am I the only person unaware that Monsieur Evariste knows the Friend of the People? I have connections, I must know these things.
MAURICE	Evariste likes to go to the Jacobins and sit on the front row making little sketches of all the speakers. One night the 'Friend of the People' asked to see them. They *are* a little partial to pictures of themselves, these Jacobins. I suppose all the mirrors are smashed.
LOUISE	They are our heroes, the Jacobins, we must have pictures of them! And Evariste's their friend! A man of surprises: not only a Patriot and a gifted artist, but a politician too.
MAURICE	He's a gifted fellow.
ROSE	As gifted as you, monsieur?
MAURICE	Oh I'm a dabbler.
LOUISE	Maurice is just a dabbler, aren't you Maurice? Maurice has been a lot of things in life but not a genius.

ROSE | You can be a genius
of dabbling, Monsieur Brotteaux, can you not?

LOUISE | A dabbler merely. But Evariste, our friend,
our fellow-picnicker, is an acquaintance
of the Friend of the People!

ROSE | You mean Dr Marat.
He's not a friend of mine.

LOUISE | He is the Friend
of the People, Sister Rose. Sister Rose
is an actress at the National, Maurice,
and thinks the world a comedy she stars in,
don't you Sister Rose?

ROSE | 'The Friend of the People'.
'The Incorruptible'. 'The Austrian Whore'.
No one's incorruptible.

LOUISE | Oh really?
Is no one a whore?

ROSE | She used to be the queen.
Call her 'Antoinette', at least it's true.
'Whore' is an opinion.

LOUISE | My opinion.

ROSE | They're creatures, they have names.
They may be vile or stupid but they're creatures.
You call them things they turn to things. You call me
Sister Rose, but I'm not
your sister.

LOUISE | Or a rose,
for that matter. Did you hear that, Maurice?

MAURICE | No, was it a riposte?

LOUISE | Just like the old days!

MAURICE | Louise, I rather agree with the young lady.

ROSE   Monsieur Brotteaux, I want you to tell me truly,
                they say in the bygone days of the Opera House
                the stars were so much lovelier to look at
                than we poor little National players now,
                is that so?

MAURICE   You would have been a star among them
                in any age.

LOUISE   She's in the chorus line.

MAURICE   Then I pity the rest of it. You'd have been a star,
                I can see you, in the myrtle grove, you are ringed
                with suitors.

ROSE   Are you there?

MAURICE   Behind a tree,
                too shy to speak.

ROSE   But it's your fantasy,
                you could wave at least.

LOUISE   One look at a painted face
                and he's far away in the long ago.

ROSE   He was,
                he took me with him.

LOUISE   Maurice, your granddaughter's
                her age.

ROSE   I doubt it.

LOUISE   Tell her what you do.

MAURICE   I hardly think it matters.

LOUISE   He's shy,
                do you want me to tell her, Maurice?

ROSE   I don't wish
                to know, if Monsieur Brotteaux doesn't wish
                to say. Do you understand that idea, Louise?

LOUISE   It's very humble work.

ROSE   I'm sure it is.
So's mine. I say twelve lines nobody says,
then someone buys me sherbet. Where were we.
Evariste Gamelin knows Marat, that little
Swiss man with a skin-disease, who'd like us
mutilated for the Nation's health.
We call him the Friend of the People.

LOUISE   For the safety
of the people, for the safety of us all,
he would remove all traitors (as would I)
all criminals of course (as would I)
quickly and humanely, for the Nation,
or would you have us in the hands of Prussians?

ROSE   Prussians, Spanish, English, Dutch, who cares
if France is one more tyranny?

LOUISE   The world
cares, the poor, the weak, you are a Christian,
Sister Rose, which side do you think Our Lord
would take?

ROSE   I don't believe He'd form a mob
and butcher priests in jail.

LOUISE   There is a state
of emergency.

ROSE   Or carry heads on pikes.

LOUISE   The heads of our enemies. What would *you* do?

ROSE   Same as the Lord would do.

LOUISE   I'm still waiting.
Come, put the world to rights.

ROSE   Oh – he'd take some loaves,
and – give them out some way and that would show us.
You're talking to a chorus girl.

LOUISE	Quite.
	Evariste knows Dr Marat. Good.
	A new connection, and that's all I'll say.
MAURICE	That's all you'll say?
LOUISE	I may be in a position
	to benefit our friend, and other parties.
ROSE	Well, Louise, you always liked a party.
LOUISE	Connections make connections.
MAURICE	Oh very good.
LOUISE	When all else fails there's wit to fall upon,
	isn't there Maurice, for one-time dukes
	and comediennes: when the Prussians come for you
	with guns and swords and there you are in a
	nightshirt,
	remember your punchline's going to need translating.
MAURICE	Louise, you are quite different to the girl
	that day in my carriage.
LOUISE	There were many days in your carriage.
MAURICE	The horse had bolted, we were thundering on,
	right to the river's edge and she grips my arm
	and cries *What's going to happen to us, Maurice?*
	But this new Louise would say *Oh, don't you worry,*
	I know this horse, I'll have a quiet word…
	Perhaps I can grip *your* arm?
LOUISE	I remember, Maurice.
	That was a foolish woman in a dream
	in a foolish world.
ROSE	The horse didn't sound so foolish.

PHILIPPE a little drunk. EVARISTE, ELODIE

PHILIPPE	Finally, full house!

LOUISE	Oh Evariste,
	the man of the hour! I do believe this
	wretch [*PHILIPPE*]
	is keeping us apart.
EVARISTE	Sister Louise,
	I'm sorry, I was working on a speech.
LOUISE	He was working on a speech! Did people hear that?
EVARISTE	Everyone hears everything.
ELODIE	Actually
	Evariste was with me, in conversation.
LOUISE	Was he indeed, well it is a day to be idle.
PHILIPPE	*I'll* decide what day it is: it's a Feast Day,
	because I say it is, and we shall drink,
	on my signal, to Equality,
	to Liberty, to Brother-and-Sisterhood,
	to France and the Revolution!
ALL	France and the Revolution!

They drink

PHILIPPE	It's Day One
	in the Month of Wine'n'Women'n'Song, and now,
	as the sun goes down and stays down,
	and the moon comes up,
	we are going…to play…a game.
ELODIE	Perfection!
LOUISE	Oh is it cards? Evariste, we two
	shall form a pair.
PHILIPPE	Louise, if you want to run things
	I'm going to have to summon you for trial
	at one of these new tribunals.
LOUISE	Are you indeed?
	Interesting you say so. I've been thinking

	about the tribunals. But I've no desire to run things. You will find me in the background.
ELODIE	Good, are we going to start the game, what is it?
PHILIPPE	I need three teams of two.
ELODIE	We'll make a team, shall we, Evariste?
PHILIPPE	This is a choice in the hands of Providence, in the hands of cards! Two hearts of blue, two hearts of white, two hearts –
ELODIE	Of red, that's like our flag!
PHILIPPE	No, is it really? The ladies to pick first, or, should I say, the Sisters…

PHILIPPE fans three cards and LOUISE picks one

LOUISE	I've a red heart.
PHILIPPE	I shall take that on trust, Louise. Clebert?

ROSE picks a white card

ROSE	White, of course. Purity. (Shut your face.)

ELODIE picks a blue card

ELODIE	I want to pick blue anyway, there: blue. Evariste, try to pick the heart that's blue.
PHILIPPE	Citizen Brotteaux.

MAURICE picks a white card

MAURICE	Now I have it the wrong way round… let me see now…white! Oh well that's lovely, chance is on our side.
ROSE	We'll make it proud, won't we, teammate?

ELODIE   Blue, Evariste, or else
                    I'm stuck with Philippe again.

EVARISTE picks a card

PHILIPPE   Whoops.

EVARISTE   It's red.

LOUISE   Evariste, you and I,
                    red hearts, red blood, blood brothers!

PHILIPPE   Bad luck there, Genius.

EVARISTE   He knows card tricks,
                    don't you? Prodigy.

ROSE   It's only a game.
                    There's only win or lose.

PHILIPPE   The Lord of Chance
                    was the judge.

MAURICE   He's all there is.

LOUISE   Before we start,
                    whatever it is, I am not permitted to know, but,
                    seeing as how the Lord of Chance has chosen
                    Monsieur Evariste to be my partner –

ELODIE   Your partner in this game.

LOUISE   In the red ranks,
                    indeed, it seems as good a time as any
                    to make an announcement to you all.

ROSE   Hurrah.

LOUISE   Now: we all know Rose made her little game
                    of Hush-don't-say-a-word,
                    let's not discuss the miracle of life
                    that's blossomed all around us, a new world
                    of Justice, of Equality, of Liberty,
                    but may I take the liberty to speak
                    on behalf of all our company, that we,

the People of France, honour the patriotism
of Monsieur Evariste Gamelin of the Section
Neuchatel. And it is my great honour
to announce that I'll be putting his name forward
for the new Revolutionary Tribunal
of that Section. Now I may not know the Friend,
as he does, but I have my own connections,
and we need men as incorruptible
as Robespierre himself! I shall recommend him
on our return to Paris.

PHILIPPE   There's a stipend,
Genius, you won't starve any more,
you'll have to change your style.

EVARISTE   I'm – lost for words.

ELODIE   A stipend? He'll be paid?

PHILIPPE   A whole new world.
Picnic's on you next week.

LOUISE   I don't expect
he'll have any time for picnics.

ELODIE   He hasn't now,
have you, Evariste?

LOUISE   Nor any time
for small talk, dear.

EVARISTE   I'm – truly, overwhelmed.

MAURICE   Perhaps you should make a speech.

PHILIPPE   Or not, you choose.

EVARISTE   Well…I thank you, Sister. I would be honoured
to serve the Revolution. These days,
are dark – dark black, black days –

PHILIPPE   That's jolly dark.

LOUISE   Hush!

EVARISTE   These are dark days there's no forgetting.
                 This world we – gave – the world, is, is threatened
                 from outside and – from inside it's – threatened.
                 If we lose this war, no one will show us mercy
                 for – doing this.

LOUISE   Hear hear!

ELODIE   Bravo!

PHILIPPE   His maiden speech! Shame we have no maidens
                 hereabouts to hear it.

ELODIE   Shut up Philippe.
                 Evariste, *men are born*, like you told the trees!

EVARISTE   Yes, yes – men are born – men are born…
                 Men are born and remain free and equal.
                 Men are born and remain free and equal!
                 Can you hear that? See those workers, in the fields,
                 they can hear me, see them turning? Long live France!
                 Long Live the Revolution! We were alive
                 to hear it cried across the fields, we were young
                 when it was said and done, when it prevailed!

ELODIE   Bravo! Bravo!

LOUISE   Hear hear!

ALL   Long Live France!

EVARISTE   The world is at war with us, war on the field,
                 not only with the Austrians, the Prussians,
                 with England and with Spain,
                 but war in the mind, in the heart, war in the
                     conscience,
                 war in the very halls of the Assembly,
                 and here we stand, alone, one Nation,
                 one People: the first ones of the world.
                 I've finished, now. Thank you.

ELODIE   Bravo, hear hear!

LOUISE   Is he not a Cicero?

ELODIE   *The first ones of the world…*it's not just trees now,
            Evariste, now *everyone* can hear you!

ROSE   Monsieur Gamelin, you are an actor
            in the grand style! We meet at last!

EVARISTE   Ah,
            but *I* write my lines.

ROSE   You've carried us away,
            it felt like '89 again!

ELODIE   I was young
            in '89, this *is* my Revolution!

PHILIPPE   Very classy, very classy. Look, Clebert,
            stick around with me, see what you get?
            New romance, new job, new eloquence,
            anything you fancy.

ROSE   Peace and quiet?

PHILIPPE   Anything but that.

MAURICE   If I might just
            add a word…

LOUISE   Oh Maurice, enough of speeches.

EVARISTE   Maurice: you must.

LOUISE   Of course, as our senior guest.

MAURICE   It's just, just a word to say
            how very proud old Mme Gamelin
            would have been today, proud of her son here,
            and if I may say, on no one's behalf at all,
            how proud indeed I am myself, of my neighbour,
            who has shown me generosity, and friendship,
            through hard times for us all, glorious times,
            but hard times, great changes,

and how glad I am that his qualities, his virtues,
will serve our Revolution. Well…

LOUISE   That was sweet.

EVARISTE   Thank you, Maurice.

PHILIPPE   Enough! By my blue heart,
                let the game commence!

ELODIE   What game? You have to tell us!

PHILIPPE opens a great dressing-up box

PHILIPPE   Charades, my little birds and bees, charades!
                Metamorphosis!
                New world, new light, new clothes,
                Red Team, White Team, Blue Team,
                Month of Meadows, Month of Heat,
                Year Two, Year One, Year Nothing!
                Dive in, my dears, new clothes, new light, we can't
                not talk about it, fine us a thousand points
                and tell me what happens next in the fucking world
                for I'm damned if I can tell you!

ACT TWO

All dance the Carmagnole

DAY V, MONTH OF HARVEST, YEAR I. Dawn. CITIZENS, including MAURICE, are queueing for bread. MAURICE takes his Lucretius from his pocket to read. MAURICE receives bread but it's snatched from him in the fracas and he returns home empty-handed, meeting EVARISTE, who has a little bread

EVARISTE   Maurice, you rose early to return
         with nothing.

MAURICE   Morning ritual of mine.
         Dream of bread, line up for bread, obtain it,
         sniff it, be robbed of it, remember it
         fondly and come home. It keeps me fit:
         I get some exercise, I take some air,
         I hear some gossip and the world I see
         is a world where no one wants to steal philosophy.

EVARISTE   Your trusty pocket atheist.

MAURICE   Then again,
         Lucretius would undoubtedly approve
         if I could trade these atoms for the atoms [*His book*]
         that form your loaf of bread.

EVARISTE   You've really nothing?

MAURICE   On the contrary I have chestnuts
         for a special treat, though such a common treat
         it might be special *not* to.

EVARISTE   Take this,
         take it, there'll be bread at the tribunal
         and I'll have my stipend soon.

MAURICE   And your dear mother
         asked that *I* look out for *you*: I promised,
         yet here I am, a beggar.

EVARISTE   Well. She never
                  accepted your…

MAURICE   My station. No. Indeed.

EVARISTE   Said she was honoured to live below a man
                  of 'culture'.

MAURICE   Well she couldn't have meant me.

EVARISTE   She did mean you, Maurice, she, she admired you.
                  I – do, you are – virtuous, despite –
                  I mean, I admire virtue, I despise
                  the accident of birth.

MAURICE   Well I'm afraid
                  that's every birth in my book, though perhaps
                  mine was among the more despicable
                  accidents.

EVARISTE   I only mean she liked
                  the trappings of – what's gone. Please have the bread.
                  Or turn it into a book, please, but take it.

MAURICE   To confuse me with a good man still remains
                  within the law.

EVARISTE   Please take it.

MAURICE   Thank you. Your first day.
                  She'd be proud.

EVARISTE   No, what she'd say is:
                  'Where's yer special togs? It don't count
                  if you got no special togs to wear!' I can hear her.
                  She'd want me noticed in the street.

MAURICE   A mother's
                  pride.

EVARISTE   She would be proud.

MAURICE   And you do have togs,
                  don't you?

EVARISTE   Yes of course, at the Tribunal
                        we wear the sash, the cap.

MAURICE   For otherwise
                        how can you divide bare-headed good
                        from bare-faced evil?

EVARISTE   Well. Thank you, Maurice,
                        for this wisdom of your – years.

MAURICE   The only wisdom that my years have brought me
                        is that the years bring none.

EVARISTE   Well they brought none
                        to France.

MAURICE   Your first day. Bravo, Citizen,
                        bring honour to our Section!

EVARISTE   I'll be late…

EVARISTE starts to go

MAURICE   Trust your heart in judgment, weigh the balance
                        there. There's all the absolutes you have.

EVARISTE   What do you mean?

MAURICE   I mean, how can a mind
                        as weak as Man's determine truth from error?

EVARISTE   By – growing stronger, purer.

MAURICE   If it were me
                        I'd roll some dice.

EVARISTE   You would abandon justice
                        to dice?

MAURICE   I would, but the spots on every face
                        would remind me nothing is pure.

EVARISTE   Nothing is pure?
                        Can nothing be made better? Can this world
                        not practise virtue?

MAURICE   Are there questions there
                you actually want answered?

EVARISTE   I'm – I'm young,
                yes, I was always called an 'idealist',
                as if to possess ideals was some option.
                But what else can you do in a world so dark
                but light a lamp? Rousseau, he lit a lamp,
                a lamp of reason, Maurice, it is reason
                that will perfect us here.

MAURICE   Oh I love reason.
                But I'm not its slave. Reason is our guide,
                it's, as you say, a lamp, but you take a lamp
                and stare at only that, you are turned blind,
                and everything beyond you is pitch black
                until the eyes recover.

EVARISTE   I love reason,
                but I love virtue more.

MAURICE   Do you love it more
                than Monsieur Robespierre? Is that permitted?

EVARISTE   My mother used to like you teasing me.
                To her I was always twelve, but I'm not twelve.

MAURICE   Well, I'm afraid I am, and I always was.
                Still can't believe how…dazzling are all things,
                all this.

EVARISTE   So you approve of how the dice
                have fallen in your case.

MAURICE   You're very sharp
                this morning, Evariste, the foes of France
                are out of luck. I only meant the world
                itself – so undeserved a gift.

EVARISTE   A gift?
                Yet you don't believe in God.

MAURICE   I'm not a slave
                to reason either, as I said.

EVARISTE   No man
                is slave to anything now. Can you believe
                you witnessed such a time?

MAURICE   I'm an old man,
                Evariste, an old man of twelve,
                and I'm a slave to that.
                And you're a magistrate
                this morning, hadn't you better go?

EVARISTE   I – yes.
                Thank you, I – don't mean thank you I mean –

MAURICE   Good
                    day.
                You mean good day.

The First Tribunal is being set up: TRUBERT sorts through documents.
RENAUDIN pours wine. Three chairs

RENAUDIN   Where's what's his face?

TRUBERT   Won't be coming back.
                They searched his house. Found what he was hiding.

RENAUDIN   What was he hiding?

TRUBERT   Don't think it concerns you.
                He won't be coming back.

RENAUDIN   I'll forget his name then.
                Fact I have already. There's efficient.

TRUBERT   We have a new man starting, recommended.
                'Gamelin, Evariste'.

RENAUDIN   Never heard of him.

TRUBERT   Nor have I and he's late.

RENAUDIN   Gamelin who?

ELODIE. LOUISE catches up with her

ELODIE   Sister Louise, your footfall is so heavy
                I thought I was going to be robbed.

LOUISE   I'm in a hurry,
                Sister Elodie, it's the first morning
                our mutual friend Monsieur Gamelin serves
                on his tribunal, I can't believe you don't know that.

ELODIE   It *is* surprising. You'd think he'd have mentioned it
                in bed this morning. Must have slipped his mind!

LOUISE   – Well. So. The pitfalls of fame.
                Do you understand his time is precious now?

ELODIE   It is, he doesn't seem to get much sleep,
                I will say that, not now he's serving the Nation.
                Would you like me to save you a seat near the front,
                  Louise?

LOUISE   That won't be necessary. He and I
                have business here this morning.

ELODIE   Oh, do you?
                Does he know?

LOUISE   Of course he knows.

ELODIE   Because your charade,
                you know, at the big picnic,
                with you as Old Europe and him as America,
                him as a teacher, you as an old lady,
                see I remember, so lifelike it was,
                that was last month, Louise.

LOUISE   There are many charades
                he'll have no time for now.

ELODIE   You should have won,
                you looked so funny. We let that old man win,
                but I think we were being kind.

The First Tribunal in session: TRUBERT, RENAUDIN, EVARISTE

TRUBERT   Nine acquittals.

RENAUDIN   Nine miscarriages.

TRUBERT   Renaudin, we voted. Three were guilty.
Nine exonerated. But we're slow.
The Popincourt Tribunal gets through forty
every morning.

RENAUDIN   Too much evidence.
You know it's cooked.

TRUBERT   I'll smell it if it's cooked.
We are too slow.

RENAUDIN   It's him, it's New-Boy here.
New-Boy, it's very simple: these are thieves
and traitors captured at the fucking Channel.
You know where the Channel is?

TRUBERT   We're wasting time.
'Citizen Garonne, J, of this Section.
Fraudulent sale of adulterated forage
to the armies of the North.'

RENAUDIN   He was caught at Calais.
Taking a little day-trip? All those others,
where's the names – Demarchais, Levecq,
then what's his face –

TRUBERT   Demay.

RENAUDIN   Philippe Demay, they blame it all on him.
Why don't we pick *him* up?

TRUBERT   We are not the police.
We are magistrates. To profit from supplies
earmarked for the military is a crime
tantamount to treason, but we need
legal proof.

RENAUDIN   We don't need legal proof,
it's moral proof, Marat's taught us that.
This man, New-Boy, was fleeing to fucking England,
to the Counter-Revolution.

TRUBERT   You can't prove that.
Acquittal. Gamelin, yours is the casting vote.

RENAUDIN   New-Boy's going to matter.

EVARISTE   I – I incline –

TRUBERT   There's death or there's acquittal.
Don't waste time.

RENAUDIN   Don't waste the poor man's day,
he's taking tea tomorrow with King George.

TRUBERT   Gamelin?

RENAUDIN   New-Boy?

EVARISTE   There is – some doubt –

RENAUDIN   Look at him, there's no doubt!

EVARISTE   And if there's doubt
we have to re-examine –

RENAUDIN   Not here,
not now, there isn't time.

EVARISTE rises

EVARISTE   Article Seven…

RENAUDIN   What is this man doing?

EVARISTE   Of the Declaration of the Rights of Man,
approved by the National Assembly of France,
August 26th, 1789, old calendar:

They have to rise

'No person shall be accused, arrested, or imprisoned
   except according to the forms prescribed by law.
   Any one soliciting, transmitting, executing, or
   causing to be executed, any *arbitrary* order, shall be
   punished.' Acquittal. I said *Acquittal.*

TRUBERT   Citizen Garonne you are free to go.
    We reconvene at three.

RENAUDIN   Christ almighty.
    Sisters of bloody mercy.

TRUBERT and RENAUDIN go

ELODIE

ELODIE   Evariste, I was there on the window-ledge,
    did you see me? Evariste,
    you were so good, so strong, so serious!
    And when you said Not Guilty and that man,
    that man he realized and his family,
    his family realized, did you see their faces?
    Did you see the children's faces?

EVARISTE   Elodie,
    it is a public court. It doesn't mean
    we watch the public, Elodie, it means
    the public watches us.

ELODIE   They were all crying,
    everyone was hugging, I felt like hugging
    all of them and saying: the man who saved you
    is my love Evariste!

EVARISTE   I didn't save him.
    Due process saved him.

ELODIE   I was just so proud
    I couldn't speak till now, my throat was all
    emotional, Evariste, you gave life!
    You gave life.

EVARISTE   Most likely to a fraud
who'll be on his way to join the Royalists
in London.

ELODIE   No no no he was Not Guilty.

EVARISTE   He was acquitted, Elodie, for lack
of proof.

ELODIE   But that's a principle!

EVARISTE   In wartime
it's a luxury.

ELODIE   I think it's still a principle.
Can I be proud of that?
Can I be proud in private?

EVARISTE   Private? There's a time and a place for private.

ELODIE   I know, dear, I was there, did you not see me,
we were innocent and guilty all at once!

EVARISTE   Don't talk about that here…

ELODIE   Or what'll you do…

EVARISTE   This is my office, Elodie…

ELODIE   Your office!
My love has an office! What can we do in an office
but talk about it?

EVARISTE   Elodie…

ELODIE   Can *I* be
next at your tribunal?

EVARISTE   You *are* next.
You'd better make your case, I've seen the warrant.

ELODIE   The warrant! What are the charges?

EVARISTE   What are the charges?
Witchcraft…

ELODIE   *Witchcraft!*

EVARISTE   Witchcraft.

ELODIE   Will anyone defend me?

EVARISTE   Not I.

ELODIE   Am I all alone in France?

EVARISTE   With your victim,
who seems to see you everywhere…

ELODIE   Oh does he…
then isn't he guilty too, and won't he have to
take the stand with me…

A knock. LOUISE

EVARISTE   Citizeness Rochemaure.

LOUISE   Citizen Patriot Gamelin.

ELODIE   Sister Citizen Brother Patriot,
it takes an hour now just to say good morning.

EVARISTE   Elodie.

ELODIE   You have business with business,
Citizen this and that. I'm not wanted
in anybody's office. (And remember,
I'm innocent, until proven *not very…*)

ELODIE goes

EVARISTE   I'm sorry, Citizeness, she's just – she's young.

LOUISE   Young in years perhaps. Did you think Garonne
was guilty?

EVARISTE   Yes. But I won't break the law
to satisfy some thug. 'Young in years…'

LOUISE   Evariste, Evariste,
my comrade from the ranks
of the Red Hearts! I do believe I've sent

a star into the firmament: my protégé
holding to his principles.

EVARISTE   This place
is not what it should be.

LOUISE   Then you will change it,
Evariste, you will stamp out corruption,
you will be strong, I saw that strength in you.

EVARISTE   I'm just one magistrate.

LOUISE   Oh in a week
you'll be Tribunal Chairman, not that tortoise.

EVARISTE   I hold to the law, Louise, but the law's protecting
hoarders, speculators, forgers, thieves,
conspirators, there's a war! On the one side
six tyrannies armed to the teeth, on the other:
paperwork.

LOUISE   Evariste…

EVARISTE   'Young in years…'

LOUISE   You'd be among the ranks
of the Patriots without my help, I know,
I'm one who smoothes the path, but I did wonder
if my meeting with our dear Friend of the People
has been arranged…

EVARISTE   It has, I forgot, I'm sorry:
go to the Jacobin Club and say my name,
he'll see you. He would like to hear your proposals.

LOUISE   The wheels are turning, Evariste.

EVARISTE   He's a good man.
His gate is never locked.

LOUISE   Now my proposals,
they may not sound so – quite so radical
as the speech of a Robespierre, or a Danton,
or – a Gamelin (did you hear, I included you

	in this pantheon of mine) but a Revolution needs resources, finances, funds, and someone has to make the right connections.
EVARISTE	You have renounced the old life, Louise, for the glory of the new: the Revolution will not forget this act. You shine a light to all the women of France.
LOUISE	The world is new, Evariste, and we must be reborn, man and woman, young and old, rich and poor. Once a Red Heart…?
EVARISTE	I'm – sorry? Oh yes, the – Picnic Day –
LOUISE	Once a Red Heart…?
EVARISTE	Always a Red Heart.
LOUISE	Always a Red Heart! Long live the Rev/olution!
EVARISTE	/Long Live the Revolution!

LOUISE goes

A knock. RENAUDIN with wine

RENAUDIN	Do I know you from somewhere, Gammel?
EVARISTE	Gamelin, I don't think so.
RENAUDIN	I sell wine. This is my wine.
EVARISTE	I'm thirsty, I'll take some.
RENAUDIN	I'm informed you're an artist.
EVARISTE	Today I'm a magistrate.
RENAUDIN	Are you. I was an artist. Not really. More a collector. I used to buy old things

53

off a man called Demay. I wonder if this Demay
cited in our case by the accused
is related to that other. They can't be brothers,
Philippe and Philippe, that's comical! Can they?
One and the same, do you think? Then I was thinking
perhaps you've come across him in the 'art world',
he always had his hand in things. But no,
you'd have 'confessed an interest'.

EVARISTE   We know no one.
We are magistrates, we are responsible
only to our consciences. The Chairman
made that clear to me.

RENAUDIN   Well I'm glad it's clear
to you, it wasn't clear to the Chairman.

EVARISTE   What are you talking about?

RENAUDIN   Seems he knew him.
Garonne, that Royalist we just let go,
we just let vanish right back into Paris.
Our Chairman's got deep pockets. There he goes now.

   TRUBERT is taken to prison

RENAUDIN   Justice in all its glory. See you Gammel.
And don't be late. *I'm* the Chairman now.

DAY XII, MONTH OF HARVEST, YEAR I

   ELODIE and PHILIPPE (at the house of Evariste and Elodie)

ELODIE   It's good of you to come, Citizen Brother.
I wasn't sure you would!

PHILIPPE   Citizen Brother,
Sister, Uncle, Greengrocer, it's me,
Elodie, it's Philippe.

ELODIE   I know it is,
I'm trying to observe the protocol.

PHILIPPE   That's very
                 sweet and romantic. Your new beau has you talking
                 like you're on his damned tribunal. *Protocol.*
                 Of course I came here, friend of yours am I not,
                 and I need to ask him something, friend to friend.
                 At the tribunal, is he?

ELODIE   He has appointments.

PHILIPPE   Fine. He has appointments. You and I
                 we used to have appointments, last autumn.
                 We didn't call them appointments, but we met
                 and went down the agenda.

ELODIE   Don't be coarse,
                 Philippe.

PHILIPPE   Coarse? Why? Wrong protocol?

ELODIE   You know my situation.

PHILIPPE   You're the friend
                 of a friend, that's everybody's situation.
                 I'll live with it. I'm sure I'm worth a laugh
                 or an anecdote at supper. Oh I forgot,
                 he doesn't eat, does he.

ELODIE   No, not really.

PHILIPPE   What does he do that men do, anything?

ELODIE   Philippe, dear, that's the point…

PHILIPPE   The point of order?
                 Can we adjourn and get ourselves a cognac
                 for the old days?

ELODIE   No. It's silly. We can't.
                 Not now.

PHILIPPE   The protocol.

ELODIE   I can't, I'm sorry,
                 it's sad this, but I can't…it can't, have happened.

PHILIPPE   What can't – what, us?

ELODIE   It's just –
             he doesn't know I was ever, that I was once,
             or we were once, and I do –
             I do have feelings for him, now, and –

PHILIPPE   All right.
             Enough, all right, I'll be, know what I'll be?
             I'll be Marseille.

ELODIE   What do you mean Marseille?

PHILIPPE   You're going to have to read the newspapers,
             sweetness, if you want to breathe the air
             he breathes. Marseille: when they took back Marseille
             from the Royalist insurgents – or they took
             a smouldering ruin – the Committee of Public Safety
             renamed it 'town with no name'. Like it never was.
             To teach it. So. Just call me Monsieur Marseille.

ELODIE   That's not the same at all.

PHILIPPE   But you'll have to teach me
             all the protocols. Have we ever met?
             Kiss on both cheeks? Do I have to be introduced
             again every hour?

ELODIE   You're teasing and it's serious.

PHILIPPE   No. I'm serious and it's lost its mind.

ELODIE   I remember you deep down.

PHILIPPE   Good. Like Marseille
             remembers the Romans, *ave atque vale*.

ELODIE   I don't know what that means, Philippe.

PHILIPPE   Well I'd tell you
             but we haven't been introduced.

ELODIE   You're just the same,
             you're always the same.

PHILIPPE   And so are you, which is strange,
                 considering what we were. Or, sorry, weren't.
                 I suddenly had a memory of a park,
                 the Allee des Veuves in August, little cottage
                 rented for the afternoon, the bloom
                 of sunset on your face –

ELODIE   Evariste! (*Is back.*)

PHILIPPE   White horses
                 off in that field, but funnily enough
                 it never happened. Must have been in the future.

   EVARISTE

ELODIE   Evariste, you're back, you're home from work,
                 Philippe is here – to see you!

PHILIPPE   You don't mind me
                 visiting your lodging?

EVARISTE   When have I ever?

PHILIPPE   Well, you know, you have an office now.
                 Genius in an office! Makes no sense!
                 Something'll have to give.

EVARISTE   You're here on business?

PHILIPPE   Doesn't seem likely does it, no, but: well.

EVARISTE   Elodie.

ELODIE   I go now,
                 see, I'm being trained!

PHILIPPE   What, like a monkey?

ELODIE   In the protocol.

PHILIPPE   Like a monkey in a costume.

ELODIE   Did you hear what he called me, Evariste?

EVARISTE   He's joking,
                it's just his style.

PHILIPPE   I'm glad someone remembers.

ELODIE goes

PHILIPPE   How was the work?

EVARISTE   I have to work with thugs.
                They'd have them all convicted to save time.

PHILIPPE   A walk, a drink?

EVARISTE   I dream
                of a walk and a drink, Philippe, but I have one hour
                then back in the bear-pit.

PHILIPPE   Genius in his lunch-break,
                and his pretty fiancée. My how the world spins.

EVARISTE   The world? More like my head.

PHILIPPE   Do you remember,
                I stood here all those weeks ago –

EVARISTE   I know
                exactly what you're going to say –

PHILIPPE   And I begged you,
                'Come to my picnic, Genius,' and you said –

EVARISTE   I know –

PHILIPPE   You'd rather mop the floor of hell
                or some such thing –

EVARISTE   And you wouldn't go away –

PHILIPPE   And so you came along and there you meet
                the girl, you get the job, and do I get
                a thank you?

EVARISTE   No, you're right, I'm terrible,
                thank you, Philippe.

PHILIPPE   It's Prodigy and I'm joking,
my style, remember, *I'm* the one who's thankful.
I'm fond of Elodie, she's like a sister,
old-style, family-style, and I always thought,
you know, she could do better.

EVARISTE   She could do better than what.

PHILIPPE   Better than, well,
sitting at home with a needle and thread and daddy.
What?

EVARISTE   If she's 'like a sister, old-style,'
then you ought to know some history.

PHILIPPE   History?
She's young, there's not much history.

EVARISTE   Of course,
she's young in years.

PHILIPPE   Well yes, that's how it's measured.

EVARISTE   What do you mean 'not much'?
I don't have long, Philippe. You're 'like a brother,
old-style', no?

PHILIPPE   She loves you, I can see that.

EVARISTE   Why shouldn't she have a history? She can love me
and have a history. Don't lie, Philippe.
You sidle through your life but you don't fool me,
not Genius.

PHILIPPE   Fair enough. There was somebody
she mentioned, nobody much.

EVARISTE   How long ago?

PHILIPPE   Years. Three years. It was nothing, he paid court,
she sent him packing, happy now?

EVARISTE   In fact:
yes.

PHILIPPE   You know, Evariste, it is your lunch-break.
This isn't a tribunal.

EVARISTE   The tribunal's
barely a tribunal, it's a shambles.
We need the new law Danton called for.

PHILIPPE   The Law
of Suspects, yes: if the Law says you're a suspect
you're fucked, do I have the gist?

EVARISTE   We are at war,
we need new legislation.

PHILIPPE   Evariste,
you're sprouting a public face.

EVARISTE   I am *called-upon*,
Prodigy, that's all.

PHILIPPE   You are called upon
now, by me, can you not be yourself?

EVARISTE   You mean: can I not be the self Philippe
is fond of? And what use was that fond self
to France?

PHILIPPE   Is that our function, old friend,
to be of use to something?

EVARISTE   To *something*?
Of use to a better world.

PHILIPPE   You know, old friend,
Genius, it's, it's insignificant
obviously, in terms of this better world,
but I hear you have a scoundrel,
Jacques Garonne, before you? I don't know him,
I know, I know *of* him, and I do know
he hates my guts –

EVARISTE   He was acquitted.

PHILIPPE   He was?

EVARISTE   For lack of proof.

PHILIPPE   Then he's the luckiest man
             in Paris. Can't imagine a different Section
             looking so kindly on him.

EVARISTE   We are bound
             by laws, and whether we like the laws or not,
             to abide by them is a virtue.
             This is the Republic
             of Virtue.

PHILIPPE   Why, 'cause Robespierre says it is?

EVARISTE   Philippe, under the tyranny, in those times,
             when we were young –

PHILIPPE   *Were* young?

EVARISTE   When we were dreaming,
             dreaming of a better world, your manner,
             your attitude to the times was the correct one –

PHILIPPE   The *correct* one?

EVARISTE   This scorn for politicians,
             suspicion of ideals, this cynicism
             yes, Philippe, but our hopes have come to pass.
             We inhabit the world we dreamed of, now's the time
             to build, not to bring down.

PHILIPPE   Is this a speech
             I pay for at the door?

EVARISTE   Your friend,
             your acquaintance, this Garonne, this speculator,
             was acquitted. You were mentioned.

PHILIPPE   But I told you,
             he hates me, he's a liar –

EVARISTE   This is not the place
             for that discussion.

PHILIPPE   Genius, I don't mix
                    with profiteers, I'm –

EVARISTE   This is not the place
                    for that discussion.

PHILIPPE   Right. I suppose it isn't.
                    I suppose it's not the place for anything.

EVARISTE   Philippe. You are my friend. We were students.
                    Now we are Patriots. Are we not Patriots?
                    Then there's nothing to be afraid of. Is there?

ELODIE comes

PHILIPPE   Got an appointment, Citizen?

ELODIE   No, I'm just –
                    it's me, Elodie!

EVARISTE   He's joking again.

PHILIPPE   No he's not.

PHILIPPE goes

ELODIE   Rose is outside. Evariste, Rose is outside.
                    Citizeness Clebert, I mean. From the National,
                    the actress. Evariste?

EVARISTE   I haven't very long. I needed to sleep
                    and now I have no time to.

ELODIE   Evariste,
                    Sister Clebert.

EVARISTE   She can wait.

ELODIE   Shall I go and tell her.

EVARISTE   She's an actress, she can – what is it – wait for her cue.

ELODIE   All right. All right Evariste. Shall I tell her to wait?

EVARISTE   She can wait to be told to wait.

ELODIE   Do you want a rest?
          Lie down, we'll rest together.

EVARISTE   You and I?
          Side by side? What kind of rest would that be.

ELODIE   I know, no rest at all!
          I've just been reading the papers, my darling.
          Do you know what they call Marseille now?

EVARISTE   There's no such place.

ELODIE   I know, I was going to say that.
          Town-with-no-name, it's called.

EVARISTE   I haven't known you long.

ELODIE   I know, but it seems
          sometimes like forever!

EVARISTE   It's, new to me, to feel this, to have this,
          this feeling.

ELODIE   It makes me dizzy when you say so!

EVARISTE   It's new to me, I say.

ELODIE   I'll always make it
          new for you!

EVARISTE   Is it: as new for you
          as it is for me? Is what I'm, what I'm asking.

ELODIE   Is it as new for me as it is for you?
          That's a bit complicated!

EVARISTE   Are there: were there:
          have there been times you felt this,
          this feeling? Other than now.

ELODIE   Other than for you?

EVARISTE   That's right.

ELODIE   No! Never!

EVARISTE   You're young, but you're full of life.

ELODIE   It's you who makes me
              full of life. It's new for both of us,
              isn't it? Like everything is new,
              the Nation, all the principles! The world's
              brand new again for us!

EVARISTE   In the course of things,
              in the course of things I learn,
              I learn there was a man, who...

ELODIE   Who what?

EVARISTE   There was once a man –

ELODIE   Sounds like a fairytale!
              Once upon a time –

EVARISTE   You can't be held
              accountable for the past. Can you.
              You didn't know me then.

ELODIE   No, I didn't,
              that's true, incredible thought, but no I didn't.

EVARISTE   So. Who was this man?

ELODIE   But – it meant nothing.

EVARISTE   Who was it who meant nothing.

ELODIE   It was – a captain.

EVARISTE   A captain who meant nothing.

ELODIE   A hussar,
              if you want to know.

EVARISTE   A captain of hussars
              who meant nothing.

ELODIE	A whole brigade of them
	means nothing when they're gone and there's just dust!
	Nothing. He was only
	fond of me, he was no one.
EVARISTE	Is he no one
	now, or is he someone?
ELODIE	I don't know,
	Evariste!
EVARISTE	Is he fighting for the Nation?
ELODIE	I don't know, I don't care!
	I can't be held – what was it –
	accountable. I won't be held accountable.
EVARISTE	Bring the actress in.
ELODIE	No, Evariste.
EVARISTE	No?
ELODIE	No.
EVARISTE	Bring the actress in *please*?
ELODIE	Yes, Evariste, I will. It is quite simple.
	I am well brought up and I love you. Now I go now.

ELODIE goes and returns with ROSE

ELODIE	Citizeness Clebert. Sister Clebert.
	I'm learning lines like you do!
ROSE	Not for long,
	not if he has his way.
EVARISTE	Go, Elodie.
	Please.
ELODIE	I leave you both to important business.

ELODIE goes

EVARISTE Hello, Rose, how are you. How's the world
       of damsels in distress.

ROSE   There is no world
       but yours, as you well know, you made a speech
       against the theatres, will you also speak
       against stories and paintings and daydreams?

EVARISTE Of course, destroy it all, you know me well.

ROSE   Is it liberty to shut down theatres?
       Is it liberty to smash up printing presses?

EVARISTE Are there questions there you actually want answered?

ROSE   Yes. There are.

EVARISTE   I can tell you've learned your speech,
       it's very good.

ROSE   Don't mock me, monsieur.

EVARISTE Oh you love the Revolution when it's all
       song and dance and solemn declarations,
       quoting Voltaire and Rousseau over coffee,
       marching in mud with all your pretty friends,
       trembling at the corpses as you tread past
       fanning yourselves for dear life, oh but now
       we're going after comedies and dumb-shows,
       and interludes and pantomimes – we're monsters!
       Poor king, poor queen,
       poor Royalists: *we only meant to change*
       the world a tiny bit so kings and princes
       would know our names and dine with us sometimes,
       but the people are taking over, the ugly, stinking
       population's everywhere – O London,
       O Rome, Vienna, save us!

ROSE   You're such a rotten actor.

EVARISTE   Give me lessons.
       I mean, until the theatres reopen.

ROSE   And what will be in the theatres that reopen.

EVARISTE   Plays, new plays.

ROSE   Plays of education,
                 instruction.

EVARISTE   Ah you're opposed to education?

ROSE   By politicians.

EVARISTE   You're opposed to them?
                 What all of them? Shall we have one godlike being
                 enthroned above us all or did we try that?
                 Think we tried that. Why have you come here?
                 You're mistaking me for someone important.
                 I don't make policy and I can't unmake it.
                 You know what was going on at your so-called
                 National Theatre. But actors were not arrested.
                 Books were not burned. Clowns were not brought to
                   tears.
                 The place was closed to be reorganized.
                 Made more accountable. Why have you come here?

ROSE   To show you a human face.
                 One that's not on trial.

EVARISTE   I know your face,
                 Rose, I admire your face, and now I've seen it.
                 And I'm sure one day I'll see it in a spotlight,
                 reciting lines it's learned, just like the old days,
                 but lines we want to hear.

ROSE   How's your lodger.

EVARISTE   I'm sorry?

ROSE   How is your lodger.

EVARISTE   Maurice? Oh yes, you played the king and queen
                 that evening, you were splendid. How's Maurice?
                 Out doing what he does.

ROSE   He's not up there?

EVARISTE   No.

ROSE   Can you wish him well.

EVARISTE   Yes. I can wish him well.

ROSE   From me.

EVARISTE   I can do that.
There's nothing else I can do. Rose. Sister.
I'll wish him well, from Rose.
So you didn't come here in vain.

ROSE is leaving as ELODIE comes

ELODIE   You will be always be welcome here,
Sister Rose.

ROSE leaves

ELODIE   What did she want, Evariste?

EVARISTE   I've no idea.
Too long ago.

He lies back and she holds him as he drifts to sleep

ELODIE   Evariste,
remember, she played the queen?

EVARISTE   There is no queen.

ELODIE   I mean, the Austrian one. I mean Austrian whore.
She was very like her. I don't mean she's – she's not,
at all, I hardly know her, Rose, that is,
not her. But I was thinking of her just now,
in prison, how – I suppose she ought to die,
the Austrian, but I thought about her children,
and maybe they didn't have to, or she could maybe
stay alive in prison and care for them,
because that would be merciful in a way.
Children wouldn't mind being in prison
if their mother was there, but look at you, Evariste,
I'm all wrong, aren't I, I'm good on the small things,

but I know I'm bad on the great things, so, in fact,
I know she ought to die because of her actions,
that woman with no name – look at your face!
I think I'm in trouble now, I'm in worse trouble
than that Austrian slut! I'm the embroidress slut
of Paris and I'm going to go in the moonlight,
tiptoe, to the border, try and make my
desperate escape! Do you recognize me?
You stop me in a village near the frontier,
you swing your lantern up to see my eyelids
and I gaze at you and I'm thinking oh have pity,
but I'm bad about the great things and it's bad
to run away, and you take me by the arms
and march me back to Paris like a prisoner.
And now I have to sit while all my crimes
are talked about in public, and my chance
to get away forever
is gone away forever.
And one night in a dream you whisper *Elodie...*
but no one has that name, so you turn over,
and sleep...sleep...sleep...

ACT THREE

DAY XXV, MONTH OF HARVEST, YEAR I

MAURICE, performing a puppet show. ROSE passing by

MAURICE   Would you like to buy a puppet for your children?
Would you like to see a show?

ROSE   No, no thank you…

She turns back

ROSE   Excuse me, am I wrong, is it not Monsieur –

MAURICE   Mademoiselle –

ROSE   The White Hearts
reunited!

MAURICE   What a joy, the White Hearts…
but here I am to the life, in my daily office
under the clouds.

ROSE   You make these beautiful figures…

MAURICE   I am indeed their Maker. I have made them
perishable, free from joy and pain.

ROSE   But look they laugh, they cry!

MAURICE   I don't know why.
I spared them from the curse of thought and feeling,
I make a benevolent God.

ROSE   And do they thank you?

MAURICE   Not a word.

ROSE   Ungrateful creatures!

MAURICE   Ah,
twas ever thus with puppets…

ROSE   'Twas ever thus…

MAURICE   So, here we are.

ROSE   You should have brought them with you,
               I mean, to that picnic.

MAURICE   Yes, but that was a day
               forgetting all our troubles. That was a day
               to forget and still, it's the only one I'll remember.

ROSE   These puppets are your troubles?
               Are they not your pride and joy?

MAURICE   Well, if you like them, yes,
               they can be my joy today, my livelihood
               can be my joy.

ROSE   I'd sooner have seen your show
               than a load of pissed charades – yours and mine
               the honourable exception.

MAURICE   Hardly fair
               to set me down beside so radiant
               a light of the modern stage. I just stood there
               and you gave your Antoinette…I was dull, I think.

ROSE   Monsieur Brotteaux, you were the toast of the night,
               and those bitches at the National sit there
               fuming that I've met you!

MAURICE   I was indulged,
               that's all.

ROSE   You were not indulged. Silly man.

MAURICE   Silly old man.

ROSE   I didn't say silly old,
               just silly. Harlequin!…and Scaramouche!
               And what about that lady, who's she?

MAURICE hides a puppet

71

MAURICE   Oh she's not finished –

ROSE   Don't put her away –

MAURICE   No please I've –
my silly pride in this and she's not ready,
she's shy, she can stay in there.

ROSE   She can stay in her shell.
I wish I were young. What? You're right. I am.
I am. So young I'd sit all afternoon
cross-legged in your theatre, with the chocolate
melting down my arm and never notice.
I'd cry out to the other children there
I know the puppet-master, he's my friend!
We were the White Hearts once in the month of what,
the Month of Forgetting. He played the king in
  heaven,
or in hell I should say, and I was his Antoinette…
'Louis, vot are you doing, vair iss your hett?'
Your line, monsieur!

MAURICE   Yes, now let me remember…
'I must have mislaid it, dear, is this the way
to the deer-hunt?'

ROSE   Word-perfect, we were the
  champions!

MAURICE   We were indeed.

ROSE   The White Hearts.
– I'm nothing now. The National's been closed.
The Committee sent a thousand
critics.

MAURICE   No more plays?

ROSE   No more of our old plays. Some new plays.
Plays they can all agree on. The Assembly's
groaning with failed writers. Have you thought

	how easily it came to them to be these watchmen over us. Anyway, I suppose…
MAURICE	You have to be going. Of course.
ROSE	To the theatre, see what's left of it. We actors always call it home, it was home for me. It made my real home lonely. Poor Clebert. I'd better steal some candles.

Two Sansculottes: BELLIER and NAVETTE

NAVETTE	Excellency!
BELLIER	Excellency, can you spare us a matinee?
NAVETTE	Is this man bothering you?
ROSE	No I'm bothering him. I'm admiring his hard work.
BELLIER	Yes it's high time you did some hard work, isn't it, your Grace?
MAURICE	We all do what we can.
NAVETTE	You're free to go, Sister.
ROSE	Very kind of my long-lost brother, but I'm talking with my friend.
NAVETTE	You are? What about?
BELLIER	It's none of our fucking business.
ROSE	Do you know, I was just now thinking that, I was seeking words that sort of expressed that sentiment, and you found them. Thank you.
NAVETTE	What's in the sack?
MAURICE	Scenery, costumes, props.

ROSE
His merchandise,
he's trying to make a living.

BELLIER
Look at this one.
You know what this one is?

ROSE
It's Polcinello.

BELLIER
I don't care what it is, what I care about
is what it looks like.

MAURICE
It's an old design.

NAVETTE
Old or young is not at this time the question.

BELLIER
It's, look at it, it's the Friend.

NAVETTE
It is the Friend.
I see what you're saying.

ROSE
What are you talking about?

BELLIER
This doll of his resembles –

ROSE
No it doesn't –

BELLIER
This doll of yours resembles the Friend, your Grace.

Doesn't it?

ROSE
It's nowhere near that ugly.
And it's got much better skin, though it's papier-
maché,
papier-Marat.

NAVETTE
You hear what she just said?

BELLIER
What's this one called?

ROSE
It's been called Harlequin
for centuries. Were you two never children?

BELLIER
This 'Harlequin', look, look it's him to the life.

NAVETTE
Him to the life.

BELLIER	The Incorruptible.
NAVETTE	This is the Incorruptible, this puppet.
ROSE	You're imbeciles.
NAVETTE	Whatever that means, we're not.
BELLIER	This aristocrat, one-time, is making puppets of heroic figures.
ROSE	You can't believe that, how can you even say it? How can you be happy?
BELLIER	Happy, lady?
NAVETTE	What's happy?
BELLIER	It's the opposite of hungry, some people say.
NAVETTE	Are you happy he does this? Makes these faces?
ROSE	Two eyes, nose, mouth, it can look like anyone.
NAVETTE	But it looks like him. It looks like – who he said.
BELLIER	Empty the sack.
ROSE	On whose authority?
BELLIER	At the polite request of the Section Force, empty the sack.

MAURICE does so, NAVETTE rummages roughly through the puppets

NAVETTE	There's more of them, you were right.
ROSE	I'm sure you'll find yourselves if you've a mind to, among the heroic figures.
BELLIER	What about that one?

The doll MAURICE hid from ROSE is a doll he's made to look like her

NAVETTE   It's a lady, very pale.

MAURICE   It's a Pierrette,
                 from an old design.

NAVETTE   'Old design', that phrase,
                 again it comes.

BELLIER   You've made this doll, your Grace,
                 now, I should say, beautiful in aspect,
                 have you not, and with a velvet mantle.

NAVETTE   I noted that.

BELLIER   And as we can all observe,
                 very pale.

ROSE   It's a *character*.

BELLIER   These figures,
                 these likenesses, depictions, these depictions,
                 are ugly, we have established your intention,
                 but this one, clearly, this one's favourable.
                 This is the Austrian woman.

NAVETTE   To the life.
                 The words were on my tongue. 'Austrian' – well,
                 'woman' was not the word.

MAURICE   It is not –

ROSE   It is not
                 the Austrian anything, as you delight
                 in calling the wretched woman –

NAVETTE   You hear?

ROSE   It's me.

BELLIER   What do you mean it's you?

ROSE   Look at it. Christ.
                 It looks like me.

NAVETTE   Why does it look like you?

ROSE   Because he's my friend. This gentleman is my friend.

BELLIER   Gentleman? What's that, a 'gentleman'?

ROSE   This citizen, this man, this old man,
                and, isn't it true, Maurice, a puppet-master
                draws faces from his life?

BELLIER   Not an old design,
                a new design…

MAURICE   It is not the former queen.
                It is not this lady, either.

BELLIER   The dead spit!
                I think this old man likes you.

NAVETTE   Love the coat…
                Can I stroke it, mmm…

BELLIER   She's whiter than you, lady.

NAVETTE   She's very white indeed.

BELLIER   There's a white cockade
                sewn on her breast. Do you know what a white
                    cockade
                means, lady?

ROSE   A white cockade, of course,
                is Royalist, but it isn't a cockade,
                it's a white heart, see the shape, do you know this
                    shape?

BELLIER   Why not a heart of red white'n'blue, lady?
                We'd pay to see that show.

ROSE   I can tell you why
                she's wearing a white heart –

NAVETTE   You mean why you are.

BELLIER   Why would we want to know? It's just a puppet,
                isn't it. A gentleman's plaything.

77

NAVETTE   I want to see a show.

MAURICE   I beg your pardon?

NAVETTE   Beg, beg, that's good.

He pushes MAURICE down among the merchandise. BELLIER restrains ROSE

ROSE   Leave him alone!

BELLIER   He wants to see a show.
           We're lovers of the theatre.

ROSE   You're filth.

BELLIER   Oh no, my lady, close:
           we *lived* like filth while he lived in a palace,
           and the whole of France was hungry,
           and you dolled up like a princess for money.

NAVETTE   Are *you* a marionette? You've got smooth skin,
              [*MAURICE*]
           but you're very large. You're going to be the hero,
           she's going to be your lover. [*'Rose' puppet*]
           There are no lines, we get straight to the action.

NAVETTE makes MAURICE 'love' the puppet

ROSE   Stop him, are you not human?

BELLIER   I'm human.
           He's human, and it's natural what he feels.
           He can express himself.

ROSE   But we've done nothing!

BELLIER   That's true, and there were things you should have
              done.
           Who's he to you?

ROSE   This isn't happening!

BELLIER   Just like a play then, isn't it, in a playhouse,
           you can sip your wine and watch it.

NAVETTE   Come on now,
             you're not too big, she's not too small, there there,
             you love the little princess, make her love you,
             make her move, she only moves when you do,
             Excellency, give us a happy ending!

EVARISTE

EVARISTE   *Stop* what you are doing.

BELLIER   Magistrate –

EVARISTE   *Stop* what you are doing.

BELLIER   Magistrate,
             we found this man –

EVARISTE   Be silent.

ROSE   Monsieur, these men, these animals –

EVARISTE   Be *silent.*

BELLIER   This man is a former aristocrat. This woman's
             an actress from the National, and the National's
             proscribed, as of course you know.

EVARISTE   Of course I know.
             There is no place for this. Help him up.
             I said help that citizen up.

NAVETTE gets MAURICE to his feet

EVARISTE   There is no place for this. Do you understand?

BELLIER   They're passing messages.

NAVETTE   With puppets.

BELLIER   Ask this
             lady what a white heart means.

ROSE   *He* [*EVARISTE*] knows
             what a white heart means, he was there.

EVARISTE   I *don't* know that.
              I know no one. There are forms, there's a Committee.
              There is no warrant out in this Section,
              not for these citizens. This man is old.
              We will have discipline.

BELLIER   The thing is spreading,
              magistrate, conspiracy is spreading
              faster than your warrants.

EVARISTE   On your way.
              The street is not the place.

BELLIER   Magistrate…
              agreed.

NAVETTE   And not agreed.

BELLIER   Agreed, but also,
              magistrate – where did the Bastille fall,
              was that in committee, was it? How do we hold
              the borders, with a pencil? – As I said,
              lady, we are lovers of the theatre,
              so I might just see you later.

ROSE   The theatre's dark.

BELLIER   Then you might not see me coming.

NAVETTE and BELLIER go

MAURICE   Evariste. Thank you.

ROSE   What was this for…

MAURICE   Rose –

ROSE   I want to know what this was for,
              this Revolution, what, I was there, I was there,
              I marched, I fought, I even had a musket
              I learned to shoot, *magistrate*, I was there,
              I wore the fucking colours –

MAURICE   Rose, Rose –

ROSE   For liberty, for equality, for justice,
              for *this*? For *them*?

MAURICE   Rose –

ROSE   We fought oppression,
              cruelty, we fought tyrants – now these bullies
              beat old men in daylight and you stand there
              calling us all *citizens* like you can't tell
              a face from a death-mask?
              Is that what you mean by *equal*?

EVARISTE   Citizeness,
              it is easy for me to imagine I don't know you.

ROSE   Is that how how it's done? Is that *discipline*?

MAURICE   Evariste –

EVARISTE   Because it's a roll of dice, you ask Maurice,
              isn't it? On a square in central Paris,
              with France encircled by the tyrannies
              of Europe, and their agents among us,
              an aristocrat and an actress well-liked
              by the old regime, consorting in private,
              and who should pass by? The only magistrate
              who – by a roll of dice – happens to know you.
              Knows, or believes, you're who you say you are.
              But roll again and I see you as they see you:
              the ones who sucked them dry and the ones who
                stood there
              giggling while they starved. You are *suspect*,
              do you not understand? Revolution
              or Treason. That is all
              you need to know, the only choice to make.
              I give this warning for – history's sake,
              that I knew you in the past.
              It's the last deed I will ever do for the past.

EVARISTE goes

ROSE   Is that it? That your speech? Do we applaud?
               Do we weep?

MAURICE   Rose, Rose –

ROSE   I have to go,
               I have to warn my friends –

MAURICE   I shall escort you –

ROSE   No – what was that cry?

MAURICE   I didn't hear it –

ROSE   Off that way, a scream. Go home, Maurice,
               promise me, bolt the door, I need to know
               you're safe somewhere –

MAURICE   At Evariste's house –

ROSE   I know,
               you're safe there, he's important, just go,
               just stay there, yes? I'll see you again, I promise!

ROSE goes. MAURICE starts clearing up his puppets

   LOUISE

LOUISE   Maurice Brotteaux, you rascal, I am *dying*
               of curiosity – was that Rose Clebert?

MAURICE   They're rounding up the actors, Louise.
               She's looking for her friends.

LOUISE   She was looking friendly
               with *you*, my dear, did you give her a puppet show?

MAURICE   Oh don't be absurd.

LOUISE   The girl's a notorious tease,
               your heart won't stand it, Maurice. What happened
                 here...
               oh dear, well, I must go, Maurice, I've business
               with Dr Marat, I have, the Friend of the People,
               a meeting with that gentleman. They say

he's ugly on the outside, but his soul
is beautiful and that makes all the difference.

MAURICE   He certainly makes a difference. He writes
that a man deserves to die, then has it printed
in a thousand pamphlets till a thousand people
are nodding over breakfast.

LOUISE   He sees all,
he sees corruption everywhere, it's true,
and it *is* everywhere. I am his colleague.
This it the Republic of Virtue,
a Nation of pure souls.

MAURICE   Was that in a pamphlet?

LOUISE   It's the truth, Maurice, the truth.

MAURICE   You'd better hurry,
in case the Doctor writes the sky is yellow
and hears you saying it's blue.

LOUISE   It is white, Maurice,
white as your head, old friend.

LOUISE goes one way, MAURICE another

SANSCULOTTES   Friends of the People, are you friends of the People
Are the foes of the People any friends of you?
Eye to the keyhole, ear to the eyehole
Somebody's doing what he's not to do
    Sing, Citizens
    O sing, Freedom
The blade is red and turns the white face blue!

*The Second Tribunal. RENAUDIN (drunk) is now the Chairman, EVARISTE
and DUPONT are the others*

DUPONT   We have no evidence this – what's his name –
Captain Maubel ever set foot in England.
Excellent army record. Citizen Chairman?

RENAUDIN　　Fine figure of a man. It's his accusers
　　　　　　want the National Razor.

DUPONT　　　　　　　　　　　We'll watch them.
　　　　　　Brother, what do you say?

RENAUDIN　　　　　　　　　　Oi, Gamelin,
　　　　　　you're being called to order, by me,
　　　　　　the Chairman, can't you see?

DUPONT　　　　　　　　　　　We two agree
　　　　　　this Captain's innocent and a patriot
　　　　　　and a soldier and we need him at the front.
　　　　　　I move for –

EVARISTE　　　　　　　Yes, indeed,
　　　　　　Captain Maubel. A patriot. Let's return
　　　　　　this man without delay to the hussars.
　　　　　　Let us send him to the frontier, for the Nation
　　　　　　in its hour of need has need of such a man.
　　　　　　Who accuses him?
　　　　　　Who accuses him?

RENAUDIN　　　　　　　　Lowlife and scum,
　　　　　　lowlife and scum, it's a conspiracy
　　　　　　but *I* know good from bad, I'm known for that
　　　　　　I am, I have a hunch, I'm never wrong
　　　　　　when I feel it in my bones!

EVARISTE　　　　　　　　　Who charges him?
　　　　　　Who points his finger at this patriot?
　　　　　　Who sullies his good name with these suspicions?
　　　　　　Who calls him traitor?

RENAUDIN stands

RENAUDIN　　　　　　　　Lowlife and scum!
　　　　　　Three cheers for Captain Maubel: Patriot!

EVARISTE　　Are we to listen to such accusations?

RENAUDIN　　No!

EVARISTE   Let us ignore them.

RENAUDIN   Ignore them!

EVARISTE   Let us ignore them all.

RENAUDIN   Ignore them all!

EVARISTE   Let's keep our fingers crossed and say a prayer,
                    oh let us patriotically ignore
                    everything! Is that what you think, *Chairman*?

RENAUDIN   I – don't – I didn't mean –

EVARISTE   It is nothing less
                    than patricide to free him.
                    It is nothing less than treason to show mercy
                    when we harbour the slightest doubt! The Revolution
                    is menaced on all sides by enemies,
                    rotted at its core by treachery,
                    in the country, in the towns, on the very benches
                    of the Assembly, even these tribunals…
                    The world awaits our downfall.
                    England is not a country. It is the Past.
                    It is the great white cliff of History,
                    the edge of Time. Because the Past itself
                    is up in arms and means
                    to annihilate us. Do you think our foes
                    can compromise with us? We have destroyed
                    the foundations of their lives – kings, queens,
                    castles, churches, slaves. If we falter now,
                    if we fail now, in centuries to come
                    people will scour the banks of the River Seine
                    to see if there ever stood a city here!
                    But who knows…he has a hunch, he has a hunch.

        EVARISTE rises and goes

RENAUDIN   Guilty!

DUPONT   The man is guilty!

85

RENAUDIN   Look he stood up already, 'course he's guilty,
            treacherous lowlife scum! I agree with this!
            I agree with Evariste Gamelin, I agree!
            Stop looking at me like that, stop looking at me!

RENAUDIN hurries out

Now the panic and confusion triggered by the assassination of Marat becomes general: flight, scuffles, arrests

LOUISE pursuing EVARISTE

LOUISE   Evariste –

EVARISTE   Citizeness Rochemaure.

LOUISE   It's me, Louise, there's a rumour of a murder!

EVARISTE   What's happening?

LOUISE   I went there as you know,
            to the Doctor's Section, to the People's Friend,
            he knows me well, but they wouldn't let me pass,
            and the rumour is he was attacked at home,
            and the rumour is by a woman, and I'm frightened.
            Evariste, we had business to attend to,
            and no one will understand, they'll see my papers,
            but you can vouch for me, we're the Red Hearts,
            can't you, I was merely well-connected,
            that's my contribution, in the background,
            at the meetings, Evariste –

EVARISTE   The virtuous soul
            has nothing to fear from truth.

LOUISE   But I'm afraid!
            Why am I afraid, don't walk away,
            a Revolution needs resources, Evariste!
            Connections, Evariste!

EVARISTE   The virtuous soul
            is without fear.

LOUISE   Wait for me, Evariste,
             remember, we were the Red Hearts, you and I!

EVARISTE goes, LOUISE barred from following by SANSCULOTTES

SANSCULOTTES   What did you vote for, why did you vote for,
               Who did you vote for, what did you mean?
               Don't ever say what you've said already
               Don't ever go where you've already been
                  Sing, Citizens
                  O sing, Freedom
               Cure your cold with Doctor Guillotine!

ELODIE, PHILIPPE

ELODIE   Citizen, I'm afraid the magistrate
             is at his work.

PHILIPPE   His name is Evariste.
             He and I were at school. I am Philippe,
             you're Elodie, and once upon a time
             we sang a fine duet, we were the Blue Hearts,
             the sun was setting, nobody expected
             such an old song from us.

ELODIE   Why did you tell him
             I knew a man?

PHILIPPE   Why? Because you did.

ELODIE   You didn't say it was you.

PHILIPPE   I don't exist,
             remember, I'm Marseille.

ELODIE   But I had to invent
             a person in my mind.

PHILIPPE   That seems fair,
             you're a person in Evariste's.

ELODIE   I said a captain,
             a captain in the hussars.

PHILIPPE   Oh glamorous,
            a dark horse and a horseman. Made in heaven.

ELODIE   You are a man of vice and you shouldn't be here.

PHILIPPE   You're a halfwit and you shouldn't be here either.
            You should go somewhere else. You should go so
                quickly
            you're there now and I'm talking to myself.
            Because I *feel* I'm talking to myself.

ELODIE   Only traitors run away, and hoarders,
            and enemies and the Counter-Revolution.
            How do I know you're not a Royalist,
            or a Girondist, or a Federalist?

PHILIPPE   You don't,
            because you've no idea what the words mean.

ELODIE   I know what a Royalist is. You might be one!
            You want me to go England!

PHILIPPE   I don't care
            where you go, but go with me.

ELODIE   Monsieur:
            I do not know your name.

PHILIPPE   That isn't true.

ELODIE   I believe in Citizen Evariste Gamelin.
            And the Incorruptible, and the People's Friend.

PHILIPPE   You believe in the People's Friend? Then you believe
            in a brand new faith. Marat's been stabbed to death.
            He's a holy martyr. Robespierre is green
            with envy.

ELODIE   He's the Incorruptible,
            and he's –

PHILIPPE   Yes, incorruptible, these names
            are very helpful. What shall we call our friend

Evariste? The Indiscriminate,
or is that one taken?

ELODIE   He's my husband now,
my master.

PHILIPPE   It's like talking to an outline,
look at you… We could call him the Rising Sun,
except, you know, the damn thing tends to set,
if anyone remembers. Rising Moon?
Same, with a sorry face.

ELODIE   You have been saying
propaganda. You were talked about
at the tribunal.

PHILIPPE   They can fuck themselves.
I've places I can go.

ELODIE   You used bad language.
You are not virtuous.

PHILIPPE   Elodie, it's me.

ELODIE   You are not virtuous.

PHILIPPE   Want to see virtuous?

He kisses her

There's virtuous.

ELODIE   Get out.

PHILIPPE   Worth the guillotine.
I have my last words ready: 'Liberty,
I may have lost you, but I took you first.'
Remember them, won't you dear, if I forget them,
you know, in all the excitement.

RENAUDIN under interrogation

RENAUDIN   Stop looking at me, you, there's not one word
the magistrate just said I'm not in total
step with, I was testing, I was testing,

I was using cunning, wasn't I? I'm known
for cunning, always was, I was known for cunning,
and I may not have the language, where's the crime
in that, I'm a plain talker, I'm a good man
and I do not want to die, in my plain language
I only tell the truth, I have a wife
expecting, I've a son, in the future,
the son of a plain man, a son of man
O God, God have mercy, hear my case,
open my case, do not conclude my case,
do not conclude my case!

RENAUDIN taken away to the guillotine

EVARISTE and ELODIE

ELODIE   Marat was stabbed! But he was the People's Friend!
              Why did they do that?

EVARISTE   Why? Because we let them.
              Because we allowed the licence of free speech
              to men who pleaded for the tyrant's life,
              and for the Austrian whore.

ELODIE   She doesn't deserve
              life!

EVARISTE   Nor will she have it
              many moments longer.

ELODIE   She's a traitor!

EVARISTE   We let them have the floor, when half their number
              had fled the country to conspire against us.
              Marat has paid the price, the very threat
              he warned us of. The time for doubt is past,
              indulgence, mercy, shadows cast by truth.
              A Captain Maubel was condemned to death
              this afternoon. I saw him catch my eye.
              I don't believe I knew him. He was a captain
              in the hussars.

ELODIE	Maubel…
EVARISTE	That's right, a handsome man, he stared at me. He was a spy for England.
ELODIE	But he's gone now, Evariste, you saw through his little scheme.
EVARISTE	I saw through everything he had ever done.
ELODIE	A spy without a secret…I can hear the rain, I can hear the rain he doesn't know is falling, he doesn't know will ever fall again, that man, that captain… You were his only hope and you looked past him into the light. Now you're *my* only hope. I'm helpless…
EVARISTE	You are alone.
ELODIE	I have to kneel before you, I'm on trial, my every word is weighed in your cold mind.
EVARISTE	The trial is long, hangs in the balance.
ELODIE	My heart beats on the door: spare her!
EVARISTE	But I'll hear no witnesses. I alone shall judge.
ELODIE	My breath is held like water in your hands.
EVARISTE	I may be thirsty, I may soon wish to drink.
ELODIE	And I'll be spilt like blood if you require it.
EVARISTE	This is the cart that takes you to the place.

ELODIE   They cut my hair,
          they tie my hands, the crowds are gathering,
          I'm trying to think of my last words!

EVARISTE   Your feet
          are climbing up the scaffold.

ELODIE   Is there something,
          anything, that can help me, is there a name
          I can say, of a nameless one, of an Enemy
          of Virtue, can I serve the Nation as I die?

EVARISTE   Thump, they lay you face down on a board.

ELODIE   For I've never known a captain of hussars…

EVARISTE   Thump, they roll you in and lock the clasp.

ELODIE   I knew a man, but he was not a soldier…

EVARISTE   Thump, and your last word?

ELODIE   *Prodigy.*

ACT FOUR

SANSCULOTTES go among the people, declaring the provisions of the Law of Suspects, a cacophony of overlapping voices

SANSCULOTTES The Revolutionary Tribunal is instituted to punish the enemies of the people, and has therefore passed the Law of Suspects.

The enemies of the people are those who seek to destroy public liberty, either by force or by cunning.

The following are deemed enemies of the people:

Those who have attempted to instigate the reestablishment of the monarchy;

Those who, by their conduct, associations, comments, or writings have shown themselves enemies of liberty;

Those who are unable to justify their means of existence;

Those former nobles who have not constantly demonstrated their devotion to the Revolution;

Those who have supported the designs of the enemies of France, by sheltering aristocracy;

Those who have sought to mislead opinion, to deprave morals and to corrupt the public conscience, to impair the purity of revolutionary principles.

The penalty provided for all offences under the jurisdiction of the Revolutionary Tribunal is death.

The proof necessary to convict enemies of the people may be material or moral.

Every citizen has the right to seize conspirators and counter-revolutionaries. He is required to denounce them as soon as he knows of them.

If material or moral proofs exist, there shall be no further hearing of witnesses.

DAY XVI, MONTH OF VINTAGE, YEAR II

EVARISTE

EVARISTE   In the old days of the Tyranny, four hundred
       thousand thrown in dungeons, cruel and capricious
       torture, fifteen thousand
       hanged, three thousand broken on the wheel,
       while the Revolution dithers to preserve
       its own life by removing a few hundred
       traitors and criminals? We create a world
       of freedom and justice, yet we hesitate
       to save it? Universal suffrage!
       Welfare assistance for the poor and needy!
       Education for all! The end of slavery!
       This is our Constitution!
       In Pennsylvania, how they rang the bells
       for freedom while the negro sat in chains!
       But his black cousins sit in our Assembly.
       A new free world, and yet you hesitate
       to save it? You say stop the guillotine?
       Then stop the Revolution! We must terrify!
       To save this world from the tyrannies we conquered
       at the Bastille, my friends, on the battlefields,
       we must terrify! To break conspiracies
       we must terrify! To counter false compassion
       we must terrify! There is a world-to-come
       of justice and equality and freedom,
       whose citizens will barely know the words,
       unable to conceive of life without them,
       but they dangle by a thread! And I assure you,
       the very second France is out of danger,
       this Terror will be over. Then our laws
       will be what we imagined in our dreams,
       and, to the virtuous man, invisible.

The Third Tribunal. EVARISTE is Chairman now

BEAUVISAGE   Carmeneau: conspiracy. Debrosse:
             conspiracy. Gilbert: prostitution.
             Silberstein: hoarding.

DUPONT   Name like that.

BEAUVISAGE   Zanette: conspiracy.

EVARISTE   Have you not finished?

BEAUVISAGE   Been at it all night.

DUPONT   There's all these piles.

BEAUVISAGE   Two more:
             Brotteaux: former aristocrat. Leclerc:
             profiteering.

DUPONT   Former aristocrat?
             Is that all we have on him?

BEAUVISAGE   'Brotteaux… Maurice.'
             He was heard to say on the day of the death of Marat
             'that Dr Marat would call the sky the colour
             yellow, if he pleased.'

DUPONT   Cross that out
             and write 'conspiracy'.

BEAUVISAGE   Look he's from your street,
             Gamelin, you better watch yourself,
             it's everywhere. Right. Send out the party.

   PHILIPPE interrogated

PHILIPPE   I told you everything, I'm a businessman.
             I supply the troops, the troops who fight the war.
             If we lose the war we lose the Revolution.
             What are the troops supposed to live on, proverbs?
             – What? What's wrong with that?
             Isn't it witty?

   ROSE. They are rehearsing

ROSE   Don't ask them questions.
                   It sounds like you look down on them.

PHILIPPE   Well it should.
                   I do.

ROSE   And don't say 'businessman', it sounds
                   British. Quote Rousseau, quote Marat.

PHILIPPE   Danton.

ROSE   No, not Danton, for pity's sake,
                   Philippe. Danton's finished.

PHILIPPE   Shit since when?
                   I can't keep up with this.

ROSE   It's the Law of Suspects.
                   It's not like the old days – like yesterday –
                   when you needed proof, and witnesses, that's all
                   gone, that's wigs and powder.

PHILIPPE   Well it always
                   did seem rather quaint, that innocent-
                   till-proven-guilty rigmarole.

ROSE   But it's you
                   it matters to. You're quick enough to help that
                   halfwit embroidress –

PHILIPPE   Elodie,
                   She's helpless, I'm not. I know some people,
                   Clebert.

ROSE   You know some people.
                   You sound like Louise Rochemaure and she's had it.
                   And you're drunk, Philippe, and you need to use your
                      brain
                   while it's attached to you.

PHILIPPE   But in my Section
                   Evariste's in charge.

ROSE   What does that mean?

PHILIPPE   Well it's Evariste, I know, but we go back.

ROSE   He doesn't *go* back, Philippe, do you not get it?

PHILIPPE   Genius, Prodigy, Prodigy, Genius!

ROSE   Oh, if you put it like that, of course, why worry,
let's go and quaff champagne at the opera.

PHILIPPE   That's a sublime idea, except the opera.

ROSE   As if there were an opera...
At least get out of this Section,
come to my place. They're so incompetent
round there they arrest each other.

PHILIPPE   And all it took
to gain admission to the holy shrine
of Clebert was the fall of the whole world.

ROSE   Of course. The last five years was just flirting.
Now it's serious. Let's get out of here.

LOUISE under interrogation

LOUISE   Of course I'm on the list, I was at the meetings,
a Revolution needs, you know, resources,
is it to live on bones? I have connections,
Citizen, I was key, I was instrumental
in several appointments to tribunals.
Evariste Gamelin was my protégé,
I'm proud to – pardon? Evariste Gamelin!
we were Red Hearts – beg pardon? Neuchatel.
You've never...I *am* sticking to the point,
I always try to – pardon? The financiers,
yes. Did I meet them? Yes. Did I meet them? No.
I'm trying to get your questions right, I'm a schoolgirl,
aren't I, I'm in trouble! Beg pardon?
Yes, he's a puppet-maker, I do know him,
it's very humble work. Did he do what?
He said the Friend of the People said the sky...
was yellow? – why did he say that – a signal?

No no, no, he said it, but he's elderly,
I'm sure he loved the Friend of the People, I know
I loved him, he was my friend, he had a beautiful
soul. Pardon? You're asking me why me,
Citizen, mister, little boy in your costume...
why me, why, I don't know...oh I don't know...

Because – because the days – because the old days...
Because the days were gold and the nights were silver.
I wore lilac at the lakeside. Why did I...
why not...Because I dressed in silk so smooth
you'd have knelt down to kiss it as it vanished.
Because you'll never have what I always got.
Because your shit is shit and mine is chocolate.
What are you looking at? You flunk, you fail,
children, stand, stand up, a lady is leaving,
I declare this meeting closed. You will not be seen.
You will not be seen, you have failed, you will go no
   further.

LOUISE taken away to the guillotine

EVARISTE at his house

EVARISTE   Today, there is a new voice, there's a –
there's a new eye, cold and calm –
new eyes – a new, blue eye...
Today there is a blue eye, cold and calm,
that looks into the corners of the State...
sees into the corners of the State...

MAURICE, unnoticed

MAURICE   'Pierces the recesses'?

EVARISTE   Oh – Maurice –
I didn't think you –

MAURICE   'Pierces the recesses'
has quite a ring to it.

EVARISTE   I didn't think –
           you were still here.

MAURICE   Still here?
           But I live here.

EVARISTE   I thought, perhaps you might –

MAURICE   Be elsewhere? Oh I wandered in the stars
           a night or two, but I settled for the earth.
           You look tired, Evariste.
           You work long hours. I wonder that so many
           foes remain at large. Is there no end
           to these conspiracies?

EVARISTE   It appears not.
           The plant is cut, the roots trail out of sight.

MAURICE   I saw whole families on their way to die.
           Three little girls white-faced and singing hymns.
           Were they signalling, do you think? Maybe to Death.
           Do you think Death's in on it? Do you think it's time
           Death trembled in a cart with a new haircut?
           Are all these plots connected, do you reckon,
           and everybody knows except a few
           incorruptibles in the dark? But of course
           you can see very well in the dark, or you can see
           what's in your mind.

EVARISTE   We know what we are told
           regarding our enemies. We do not torture
           in the Virtuous Republic, that is a vice
           of tyrannies.

MAURICE   There are some who might believe
           that putting a man to death is itself vicious.
           Five years ago this was the opinion
           of a lawyer named Robespierre.

EVARISTE   Our enemies
           have given us no choice. There is virtue
           or there is death.

MAURICE   Is everything two-sided,
Evariste? Can you truly see a line
bisecting all the world? I may believe
the world an accident, but I still observe
infinities of colour.

EVARISTE   Atheism
is not a virtue.

MAURICE   No, but it's a right,
is it not? I should imagine God Himself
would recognize that right.

EVARISTE   You make no sense.

MAURICE   Another right He recognizes, or,
would if He existed.

EVARISTE   He exists,
not a tool of Romish priests in their palaces,
but the Supreme Being of the common folk.
It is a vice to doubt what the Nation knows,
to ridicule the faith of the sovereign People.
The man of incorruptible virtue
has called for a Festival in celebration
of the Supreme Being.

MAURICE   Oh, do they share a birthday?

EVARISTE   He has set aside the personal for the sake
of the Revolution.

MAURICE   No, what he's set aside
is the Declaration of the Rights of Man.
I hear it hangs on a wall at the Jacobin Club,
shrouded in black cloth.

EVARISTE   Who told you that?

MAURICE   I read it in a paper.

EVARISTE   Which paper?
There can be no papers till the war is over.

They fuel our enemies. When our enemies
are broken it will cease,
this terror, we will lift the Law of Suspects
and turn our Constitution into law.

MAURICE   And the Supreme Being will ascend his throne.

EVARISTE   There are no thrones.

MAURICE   Then where on earth will he sit,
poor Monsieur Incorruptible?

EVARISTE   He is not
the Supreme Being, he is our guide through danger.
One man must light the way.

MAURICE   Must it be one
who knows no other way?

EVARISTE   Neighbour, I must ask you, you have been,
always, for my mother's sake, always,
a friend to me…I must ask you why it was,
why it was you said, you were heard to say,
on the day of the death of Marat, that he would say,
Marat, the sky was yellow, why it was,
that you said that. As a citizen I ask that.

MAURICE   I don't remember saying that at all.
I'm an old man. Was it rude?

EVARISTE   For my mother's sake,
for my mother's sake I mention to you now,
neighbour, that it's known that you said that.
People will want to know why you said that.

MAURICE   People? Or *The* People. Because people,
Evariste, I always got on well with.
The People, now, that's new to me, that notion,
that so many think the same. I don't believe
I ever met two *men* who thought the same,
let alone a population.

EVARISTE   You were an aristocrat. You were a duke.
              The law requires that you explain yourself.

MAURICE   Explain why I was me?

EVARISTE   For my mother's sake,
              I mention that the time is short,
              they're searching this whole street,
              they are going to ask that question when they reach
                here.
              My mother, sir, loved you, and for her sake
              I mention to you –

MAURICE   Sshh…

EVARISTE   I – beg your pardon?

MAURICE   Sshh…
              She isn't there, my friend. She cannot see,
              she cannot know. She is returned to dust,
              to atoms, Evariste, there is no one here
              but us, at night, on earth. You are free now,
              to be this man you are.
              It pains me to see you trying to be a son.
              You are no one's son. You are all alone in your life.

EVARISTE   Citizen – Brother –

MAURICE   Sshh…

Loud knocking at the door

EVARISTE   Neighbour – Maurice –

MAURICE   Sshh…
              I have my book. I shall go to meet The People.

MAURICE goes to give himself up

ROSE and PHILIPPE

ROSE   Philippe, I can see them at the crossroads,
              they're looking down this street.

PHILIPPE   They're theatre-goers,
              they probably want a piece of you. Anyway,
              you said I was safe out here.

ROSE   Why do you think
              you're safe anywhere?

PHILIPPE   Because you said I was,
              Rose, and you're my queen.

ROSE   Don't call me Rose.
              Call me Clebert or it's not the world I know.

PHILIPPE   Rose…

ROSE   We are best friends, have you lost your mind?

PHILIPPE   My mind, my head, who's going to notice now?

ROSE   They've gone.

PHILIPPE   See? We're quite anonymous,
              left to our affairs.

ROSE   You distracted me,
              I didn't see where they went. Just when I needed
              sense from you, Philippe, I get this horseshit.

Knocking nearby

ROSE   That's them.

PHILIPPE   You said they'd gone.

ROSE   I said I couldn't see. You have to go,
              over the wall, now.

PHILIPPE   The wall – then where?

ROSE   To the forest, fool.

PHILIPPE   What will I do in the forest?

ROSE   Survive, Philippe.

PHILIPPE   But I'm a city boy,
                    Clebert, I'll never make it, what do I eat?

ROSE   Go, Philippe!

PHILIPPE   Come with me, we'll be like
                    Adam and Eve, like the world got so vile
                    God lets us start again.

ROSE   I'm staying here.
                    You're leaving. Go to where we had that picnic,
                    with the game and the cards, the little stream,
                        remember?

PHILIPPE   What am I meant to do there, hunt rabbits?
                    There won't be any left, half the Assembly's
                    hiding in the forest.

ROSE   I'll find you.

PHILIPPE   I don't want to go, Clebert, I mean, *you're* here,
                    and I know it's me but I love you in my style,
                    and it's all I have, do you hear me?

Knocking on their door

ROSE   Go! Go down the stairs!

GUENOT and DELOURMEL

GUENOT   Rose Clebert, actress?

ROSE   What?

DELOURMEL   Rose Clebert: actress.

ROSE   No.

GUENOT   You're Rose Clebert the actress.

ROSE   Rose Clebert.
                    Not the actress.

GUENOT   Formerly the actress.

DELOURMEL   So who are you?

PHILIPPE   I'm…Philippe. Philippe.

DELOURMEL   It doesn't say you live here, Philippe-Philippe.

ROSE   He doesn't live here, do you. He was leaving.

DELOURMEL   Finished his business, has he.

GUENOT   You: be quiet.
                It's just procedure. We know who you are.
                You're known to us, but we do have a procedure.

ROSE   All right. What is the procedure?

GUENOT   That you come with us, to the Section.

ROSE   Any reason?
                Or just social.

GUENOT   For a reason.
                He can go.

DELOURMEL   Can he go?

GUENOT   Unless you want him
                along with you.

ROSE   I don't. He's nobody.

DELOURMEL   Are you nobody, mate?

PHILIPPE   Yes. I'm…nobody.

DELOURMEL   So you don't mind what we do? [*To PHILIPPE*]

ROSE   No he doesn't mind.
                I mind. God minds.

DELOURMEL   You don't mind what we do?
                [*To PHILIPPE*]

PHILIPPE   No…I don't mind.

DELOURMEL   That's good. Are you nobody?

PHILIPPE   Yes.

DELOURMEL   Just checking your status.

GUENOT   He can go.

DELOURMEL   You can go. And you really don't mind what we do?
              Shake your head for no, nobody.

PHILIPPE shakes his head and goes

DELOURMEL   We're alone now, with a beautiful young actress.

GUENOT   Who are the White Hearts, lady?

ROSE   What did you say?

GUENOT   Who are the White Hearts?

ROSE   It was a – it was a picnic.

GUENOT   Why white?

ROSE   It was a picnic, we picked cards.

DELOURMEL   Picked them on a picnic.

GUENOT   Be quiet.
              Do you know the Duke of Ilettes?

ROSE   There is no such thing
              as a duke of Ilettes.

GUENOT   Do you know Maurice Brotteaux?

ROSE   No.

DELOURMEL   Alone, with a beautiful young actress.

ROSE   Stop saying that.

DELOURMEL   Nobody knows we're here.
              Only that man and you heard that man admit
              he's nobody. So nobody knows we're here.

GUENOT   Be quiet. We know we're here. These are the Days
              of Virtue. Let's go, lady.

They escort ROSE away to prison

EVARISTE in his lodging

EVARISTE   Today there is a blue eye, cold and calm,
            piercing the recesses of the State,
            to prise out enemies with a force and insight
            never seen before –

ELODIE, painted and costumed as 'France'

ELODIE   Look upon me, magistrate. Do you know me?

EVARISTE   I know you. What do you say?

ELODIE   What do I say…

EVARISTE   Time and space, where are we?

ELODIE   Day 26, the Month of Vintage.

EVARISTE   The year?

ELODIE   Year Two.

EVARISTE   Who are you now?

ELODIE   I am the Sovereign People.
            I recognize the Supreme Being and the immortality of
              the soul.
            I recognize that to worship the Supreme Being I
              must –

EVARISTE   Practise the duties –

ELODIE   Practise the duties of man.

EVARISTE   Who are you, what do you hate…

ELODIE   I am Liberty, so I hate bad faith and tyranny.

EVARISTE   What are you, whom do you punish…

ELODIE   I am Vengeance, so I punish kings and traitors.
            I am Brotherhood, so I help the poor, the weak, the
              old, and the oppressed. I am Virtue –

EVARISTE   What do you do?

ELODIE   I am Virtue, so I do to others all the good I can.

MAURICE in prison, reading his Lucretius

ROSE, LACROIX

LACROIX   You. There's a prisoner here from the female section.
              You have five minutes.

ROSE   Maurice, Maurice, it's me.

MAURICE   Why Rose, what a, a joy for me to see you,
              but horror for you, why you?

ROSE   I've been denounced.
              Played too many princesses. I did try
              explaining what a play was, and a costume,
              but I think my judges only liked the circus.

MAURICE   Why have they let you come here?

ROSE   They wouldn't,
              but the prison warden knew me in my glory,
              so we had this little bargain,
              and, he let me. Maurice, he told me,
              they're going to search the cells, they'll take your
                book,
              your what-is-it, Lucretius, give it to me,

MAURICE   He's been with me forever.

ROSE   They'll take him *from* you
              forever, or I'll keep him for you forever.
              I mean, until –

MAURICE   Keep him then, and keep this.
              [*A bible*]

ROSE   What's this?

MAURICE   There was a priest,
              and this is all that's left of him.

ROSE   It's a bible.

MAURICE   Yes, but it's a book as well, and books
ought to survive us if they're worth the writing.

ROSE   Did you – look into this book?

MAURICE   I may have glanced,
Rose, it hasn't changed, an eternal being
who sees what we get up to, and who cares –

ROSE   Maurice, He cares, my dear –

MAURICE   Yes He's very busy,
but He'll catch us when we die –

ROSE   Maurice, He will –

MAURICE   And give us life forever in the clouds.
I like a storybook, a book at bedtime,
it's read to you, you sleep, you...

ROSE   Maurice, Maurice, my white heart, it's all right,
I'm here, your books are safe, when you get out
we'll read them both together, you and I,
the one you believe and the one you don't, that's fair,
isn't it –

MAURICE   I'm about to die, you know.

ROSE   You're not about to die.

MAURICE   Don't tell me lies,
Rose, like that book, don't tell me lies
like priests, don't tell me lies
like kings and revolutionaries, don't tell me
little things you think will be some help.
Tell me something hard and unconsoling,
tell me a useless fact I can cling on to
tonight, all night, tell me a cold dark thing
that can't be altered.

ROSE   I have one: I love you.

MAURICE   The sweetest of all lies, of course she does,
she loves all creatures, she can't help herself,

                she sees a thing and all she can ever think of
                is help this poor –

ROSE   You clueless, hopeless man,
                I love you, I want you, there's your cold hard
                useless fact delivered. Can I go now?

    They kiss

                Maurice, I still have friends in the Assembly,
                the writers there, no one knows what's coming,
                there's a faction against Robespierre – if he falls,
                who knows, I can help you darling –

MAURICE   Rose, do nothing,
                nothing.

ROSE   What are you mad?

MAURICE   Rose, Rose Clebert,
                do nothing.

ROSE   No!

MAURICE   Do nothing, do not speak,
                do not write, do not petition, ask nothing
                of anyone, I beg it of you, Rosie.
                Safety lies in silence. Safety lies
                in time, Rose, let time begin its work.
                It cannot hold, this horror, it must end,
                Rosie, Rosie Clebert, Rose Clebert,
                the forgotten will survive. Be the forgotten.
                Do what I say, and I'll die happy, knowing
                I saved you –

ROSE   It's not so, don't even say it –

MAURICE   I'm done for, little child.

ROSE   I'm not your child,
                or little, I'm your lady –

    LACROIX

LACROIX   That's enough.
                    You have to go. Do you have books, excuse me?

ROSE   Excuse me, yes I do.

LACROIX   He's not allowed them.

ROSE   He hasn't got them, *I* have, excuse me.
              I love you, Maurice.

LACROIX   Enough.

MAURICE   Rosie, do nothing.

LACROIX   She's welcome to do nothing.
              Nothing's what she can do.

ACT FIVE

The Calendar is changed to DAY IX, MONTH OF HEAT, YEAR II. Female SANSCULOTTES pass by, costumed as Elodie was

SANSCULOTTES   Men called Robespierre are all born equal
                     Men called Robespierre are freedom's few
                     Men called Robespierre will sit in judgment
                     Men called Robespierre are watching you
                       Sing, Citizens
                       O sing, Freedom
                     Bet you wish your name was Robespierre too!

Gunfire, explosions far off

PHILIPPE interrogated

PHILIPPE   Am I a what? A Federalist? No,
                  I'm nobody. A Dantonist? Fuck that,
                  I'm nobody, I'm an ordinary man,
                  sir. Where are my papers? I was assaulted,
                  I was set upon by an aristocratic gang,
                  I was…do I believe in what? Oh I do,
                  yes, it's Supreme, it's very Supreme indeed,
                  and I believe in – it. I'm with Rousseau
                  on that one, yes, and Marat, holy martyr,
                  God rest his – Supreme Being rest his soul
                  I loved that man. Not like that bastard Danton.
                  What a bastard, eh, saw clean through that one.
                  Am I a what? You asked me that already,
                  I'm nobody, citizens, I love my Nation!
                  You found me on the street – I'm the man on the
                    street!
                  I agree with everything you want me to!

ROSE asleep in prison. Two guards: CHALIER asleep, JAVOGUES eating bread

JAVOGUES   Can't move in the street for them,
                  fans of the charming actress.

They want to know some stuff about your art-form,
before it's too late.

ROSE   Is any of that for me? [*Bread*]

JAVOGUES   They want to know, is it tiring, your art-form?
having to do it every night, for money,
doing it in the afternoon, is it tiring?

ROSE   I wouldn't mind some bread.

JAVOGUES   She wouldn't *mind*
some bread, but prefers cake. Does it make you
   hungry,
your art-form? Does it makes you sweat? I've a
   speech.
I say it and then you.

ROSE   I know, we've done this
every day for weeks, I'm so excited.

JAVOGUES   Then, you might get some bread.
Repeat, after me: I do it every night.

CHALIER   Shut up, I'm trying to sleep.

ROSE   Have we started?

JAVOGUES   I do it every night.

ROSE   I do it every night.

JAVOGUES   I do it for you my darling.

ROSE   I do it for you my darling.

JAVOGUES   (Look at me when you say that.)

ROSE   Look at me when you say that.

CHALIER   Ha, she got you there.

JAVOGUES   No she didn't.

I'm doing it right now.

ROSE   I'm doing it right now.

JAVOGUES   I love to do it with you.

ROSE   I love to do it with you.

JAVOGUES   And now I have earned my bread.

ROSE   And now I have earned my bread.

JAVOGUES   My fucking bread.

ROSE   I have earned my fucking bread.

> *JAVOGUES throws her some*

CHALIER   Stop doing that stuff to her.

JAVOGUES   She enjoys it.
                She does it for a living.

> *Cannonfire*

                What the fuck was that?

CHALIER   That was closer.
                Go and see what's going on. And don't get killed
                or I'll have to stay awake.

> *JAVOGUES goes*

ROSE   Can I have more bread. Please.
                Thank you. Out there… Is it the Austrians?

CHALIER   There are no Austrians. There are no Prussians.
                There are no Dutch. There is no world. Just us,
                just waltzing with ourselves. What does it matter?
                It won't be long for you now. Don't worry,
                it comes and then it's over. You don't know
                it's over, for it's over. That's the mercy
                of God.

ROSE   The Supreme Being.

CHALIER   I know His name.
                He knows my name.

ROSE	Yes, He knows your name. Do you pray to Him?
CHALIER	Well. Who else is listening.
ROSE	Will you tell me when you do?
CHALIER	You'll notice.
ROSE	Then I'll watch you.
CHALIER	You'll watch me?
ROSE	Who else will?
CHALIER	No one. Eat, lady. Watch me while I'm sleeping.

More gunfire. Panic, fighting among SANSCULOTTES

EVARISTE at home, smartly dressed, rehearsing a speech

EVARISTE The Incorruptible has shown us evil
in the form of compromise and he has shown us
evil in the form of excessive zeal…
The Incorruptible has shown us evil
in the form of moderation, and of zeal…

A knock

Yes? Who's there? Who is it?

PHILIPPE, bleeding, ragged

What are you doing here?
You're bleeding, are you – all right – are you on your
way?

PHILIPPE Yes. They said, out there,
five minutes.

EVARISTE This is unusual, this is
irregular. I can't – *do*…anything.

PHILIPPE I know –

EVARISTE For you –

PHILIPPE   I know that –

EVARISTE   This is highly
                    irregular. Why have they let you come here?

PHILIPPE   We were – friends, I said to the guard, you and I were
                        friends
                    in the old days and the guard said: five minutes.

EVARISTE   In the old days. Would you like the old days back?

PHILIPPE   The old days? There were old days in the world,
                    Evariste, as you say, there was tyranny,
                    yes, but *we* had old days, we had old days
                    too and I sometimes, think of them as good days,
                    you and me, smell of the paint on a hot day
                    in that studio we shared…to hell with school
                    let's stroll along the river, sit in the park,
                    watch the girls go by. Those were the old days.

EVARISTE   You're white as a ghost. You're the shade of the old
                        days.

PHILIPPE   I *am* a ghost, look through, you see there's nothing:
                    space. I was your friend.

EVARISTE   This is insane.
                    They know what happened to Marat, there've been
                        attempts
                    on Robespierre himself –

PHILIPPE   I'm not armed,
                    for Christ's sake, Evariste, I've nothing left.
                    I went home, there was nothing, I was, I was,
                    I was with Rose when they took her, I was there,
                    and I wasn't there…and Elodie? Evariste,
                    can you tell me where she is?

EVARISTE   Elodie?
                    She's serving the Republic. *Prodigy.*

PHILIPPE   Genius…

EVARISTE   Look at you.

PHILIPPE   Why.

EVARISTE   To see the old days
drowning in the new.

PHILIPPE   Are you going to sketch me?
For the old days?

EVARISTE   I don't need to.

PHILIPPE   Five seconds you could sketch me. One second.
Give me the blank sheet back and there I am,
in all my – to the life…to the life.

EVARISTE   Whatever – transactions – you engaged in,
you must explain them, not to me, not now,
but to the Prosecutor. I am sure
justice will prevail.

PHILIPPE   I'm not so sure
justice knows what's going on. The law
is death to every outlaw – maybe justice
was one of those.

EVARISTE   There is virtue, there is death.

PHILIPPE   Is that our portrait? *Picture of Death and Virtue*?
It will hang somewhere and children of the future
will wonder: Death and Virtue? Which is which?
They both look very white.

EVARISTE   You understand,
Prodigy, you understand. And the future
will understand. You that we condemn,
you climb the scaffold, passing from a world
too virtuous for you, into a realm
where all will be forgiven. People say
the eyes are bright at the end. And in your eyes
I see that strength.

PHILIPPE   Evariste…

EVARISTE   You go to Paradise, but you depart
a new Jerusalem: universal suffrage,
education, welfare for the poor,
an end to slavery, freedom of the press,
peace to all mankind –

PHILIPPE   When will those laws
be passed, my friend?

EVARISTE   When we are out of danger.

Distant cannonfire

PHILIPPE   Genius, can you hear the guns?

EVARISTE   The Past
still fighting to be heard. We will destroy it.

PHILIPPE   Where have you been all day? Where's Elodie?

EVARISTE   I have set aside the personal.

PHILIPPE   Where is she?

EVARISTE   I cannot associate with vice.

PHILIPPE   Evariste,
for God's sake, she's your wife.

EVARISTE   Is it a riot?
The National Guard will deal with them. And still
they doubt there are conspiracies, the Nation's
rife with treason –

PHILIPPE   You've not set foot outside,
have you?

EVARISTE   I was resting, I was tired,
I was excused my work at the tribunal,
I wrote a speech, I'm going to have it printed
and sent to Robespierre –

PHILIPPE   Then you'd better hurry.

EVARISTE   You'd better hurry, Prodigy, if there's some
           last truth you'd like to tell me, some last
           truth about the old days.

PHILIPPE   There's no time.

EVARISTE   They said you could have five minutes.

PHILIPPE   They said *you* could have five minutes.

EVARISTE goes to the door and comes back

EVARISTE   Those aren't – the men who were there.

PHILIPPE   They are now,
           Genius, they're the men who are there now.

EVARISTE   There…now…there now.
           Of course. There now.
           So it comes. It comes.
           He said the day would dawn,
           the Incorruptible – this is insane –
           those aren't the men who were there…
           But of course, he said, he knew it was coming, he did,
           they tried to shout him down, he knew they would,
           he knew it was planned, those failed preposterous
             playwrights,
           he knew they were traitors, what have they done,
             where is he?

PHILIPPE   Robespierre, where is he?

PHILIPPE   Well he's lying, since you ask,
           since you care, in a lake of his own blood.

EVARISTE   Did he – by his own hand? What did he do?

PHILIPPE   He shot himself in the jaw, he was half-successful.
           A bloody mess, you know, to be half-successful.

EVARISTE   Universal suffrage, education,
           welfare for the needy –

PHILIPPE   Abolition
                   of death itself and sweets for evermore.

EVARISTE   I have to leave.

PHILIPPE   You do,
                   old man, you're on a list of his disciples.

EVARISTE   Prodigy –

PHILIPPE   Evariste, where's Elodie?

EVARISTE   Prodigy, there's a cloth, there's a black cloth
                   at the Jacobins, it covers the Declaration –

PHILIPPE   Look at me, where is she?

EVARISTE   You must go there,
                   you must take it down, you must show it to them all,
                   the Declaration of the Rights of Man,
                   you must take it to the Assembly and show them:
                   this is the thing we gave the world!

PHILIPPE   Where is she?

EVARISTE   Where is she, where is she…
                   the light blows out and still he asks
                   where is she, where shall we dine, where shall we
                      dance,
                   where shall we fuck –

PHILIPPE   Evariste –

EVARISTE   The light blows out,
                   Virtue snuffed and Reason strangled, earth
                   goes spinning backwards into the bowels of tyrants
                   as he wonders where shall we lunch, where shall we
                      breakfast?
                   There will be men like you
                   forever, free to be this-and-that at leisure
                   till tyranny tracks you all and you wake one morning
                   chained to each other. Philippe. Take my hand.

PHILIPPE   What?

EVARISTE   I am going to die, you are my friend,
                   take my hand, that's good.

PHILIPPE   Well I do believe
                   I know you, are you that Evariste Gamelin
                   I was at school with?

EVARISTE   The Evariste Gamelin
                   you lit the flame with, walked the earth with, oh,
                   Philippe, it will be so beautiful –

PHILIPPE   Old schoolmate –

EVARISTE   When it comes, when it comes one day –

PHILIPPE   Old Genius,
                   you're tired –

EVARISTE   I'm cold, Philippe, I'm cold as marble.
                   This is my speech, they will engrave this on me,
                   you must read it to them, Prodigy.

PHILIPPE   No, Evariste,
                   you keep it. You can read it
                   to the People.

EVARISTE   Yes, that's right,
                   over the heads of traitors, to the People.

   EVARISTE goes to be arrested

PHILIPPE   Hello…is there…someone?

   ELODIE emerges, smeared with paint, confused

PHILIPPE   Elodie, oh my girl…

ELODIE   I am Liberty, I am Justice, I am France.

PHILIPPE   Elodie, my girl…

ELODIE   I am No-Girl, I am No-Girl,
                   I am Girl-With-No-Name.

PHILIPPE   Elodie, you are Elodie,
                  look at me, it's Philippe, Philippe Demay…

ELODIE   You are not virtuous. And I am Virtue,
                  I am Liberty, I am France!

PHILIPPE   You are Elodie,
                  and what have you been taking – Jesus Christ –

ELODIE   I am Vengeance, I am Justice!

PHILIPPE   You're a little girl,
                  angel, an embroidress, it's over,
                  Elodie, be still now, be still now…

ELODIE   Nine, the Month of Heat, Year Two.

PHILIPPE   July, angel, 1794.

ELODIE   I am the Sovereign People…

PHILIPPE   Hush now.

ELODIE   I am Brotherhood and so I help the poor,
                  the weak –

PHILIPPE   The old.

ELODIE   The old –

PHILIPPE   And the oppressed.

ELODIE   And the oppressed…

PHILIPPE   And that is beautiful,
                  Elodie, it is beautiful to do that,
                  we'll do it together, won't we, but we go now,
                  we go to somewhere safe…

ELODIE   And do to others
                  all the good we can.

PHILIPPE   And do to others
                  all the good we can.

He leads her away

EVARISTE on his way to the scaffold

EVARISTE   So it is now as always,
as it was before: the man of purity
falls by the hand of treason,
dies in the midst of thieves,
and the Virtuous Republic is no more.
The Incorruptible, too good for this world,
has left it now for the Supreme Embrace,
and shrunken men disgrace the halls of power…

His cap is taken from him

And you will enjoy for centuries to come
the liberties we died for. You will stroll
the skyways of the future without kings,
without lords or dukes or servants, without slaves,
without chains, but with these things,
these simple, precious things:

His jacket is taken from him

shelter for every citizen, a voice
for every adult, and for every child
an education, justice for all men,
all women of all races, all equal
in the sight of the Supreme Being. Now,

His shirt is taken from him

oh now you laugh to see me
as I am. I am a sacrifice
to that just future. And you will laugh as others
fight for justice, you will joke as others
die for truth, and duck your head as others
bleed for their liberty. You will live in Eden
one day and you will curse it to the last
petal.

His hands are tied

> Blessed Terror, Holy Terror,
> for Freedom and Equality and Brotherhood
> we die! I am Evariste Gamelin of the Section
> Neuchatel, I am Evariste Gamelin!

He is led away to the guillotine

This is 'Thermidor' – the Jacobins have fallen and the Terror is over. The Revolutionary Calendar is torn down. MASKED REVELLERS celebrate

ROSE makes her way home, clutching her two books. She sits at a little table and reads

REVELLERS *Off with your head and on with your head-dress*
Out of your skulls and sleep till dawn
Drink till you're free and fuck till you're equal
Anything goes now everything's gone
 O dance Citizens
 O dance Freedom
Raise the dead and paint their faces on!

REVELLER Citizeness Clebert of *le Théâtre Nationale,* we have found you at long last!

REVELLER Citizeness Clebert of *le Théâtre Nationale,* you cannot hide from us!

REVELLER Citiziness Clebert, Rosemarie,
actrice, comedienne, bonne viveuse
you are hereby accused
of the following heinous crimes: that you did
wilfully absent yourself from those
who love you!

REVELLER   Who have loved you many times
in the gardens of *Paree!*

REVELLER   The Rose gardens,
the Rose meadows, the Rose countries, the
 Rose worlds...

REVELLER   You are furthermore hereby accused of crimes
            against the state…of fashion, look at you!
            and are condemned…to dance! Rise, Clebert!

This REVELLER *is* PHILIPPE, *who removes his mask*

ROSE   Clebert…

PHILIPPE   For the love of God where have you been?
            I come here every night and you're never here!

ROSE   I'm here now.

PHILIPPE   I asked at all the prisons,
            I went round fucking graveyards for you,
            I even tried the National, I had to
            sit through something, oh and I tried the place
            we had that picnic? That's where you said you'd be.

ROSE   I didn't think I would be, though, Philippe.

PHILIPPE   No.

ROSE   And see? I wasn't.

PHILIPPE   No. We are not the – people we were. We're better!
            Don't you miss us all, Clebert? Don't you miss me?

ROSE   Not now you're here.

PHILIPPE   And look who else is here…

PHILIPPE *opens all the doors, to reveal the* REVELLERS. *He draws one
forward:* ELODIE, *who takes off her mask. She wears a red neck-cord*

ELODIE   My poor old Sister Rose. Home again now.
            Remember when we met? Philippe and I,
            we were the two Blue Hearts! Look I wear this cord,
            you see, so I don't forget. Look, you've got one.
            Who's yours in memory of?

PHILIPPE   It's all behind you, isn't it, Elodie,
            the bad times.

ELODIE   It's all behind me, Rose.
                 We're making a brand new start.

PHILIPPE   Clebert, Clebert,
                 is this a part you're learning?

ELODIE   It's very long.
                 Are you making a comeback, Rose?

PHILIPPE   Not tonight!

ELODIE   We're taking you to a party!

ROSE   To a party...

PHILIPPE   Remember them? Now, see this book here, now
                 gently see we close it, 'Lucretius',
                 and this one's very sleepy, very old,
                 then we take the lady's hand...

ROSE   Just – a moment.

PHILIPPE   We want you back. You're coming to a party.

ELODIE   Allee des Veuves, by the river!

ROSE   Allee des Veuves...
                 I've nothing to wear.

ELODIE   I'll find you something! Please,
                 we need you back, so things are like they were.

ROSE   I look a fright.

PHILIPPE   You think these people care?

ROSE   No I don't think they care.

PHILIPPE   Then come *on*!

REVELLER   Arrest that Citizen, she's got no wine!

REVELLER   Stick her on trial, the woman's stone cold sober!

PHILIPPE   Go on, you wretches, she'll come along with us.

The REVELLERS depart

My carriage awaits.

ELODIE   *Our* carriage, yours and mine,
                 Rose.

PHILIPPE   Well, it awaits,
                 sisters, and it won't be waiting long.

PHILIPPE goes

ROSE   Will you sit with me, Elodie,
                 by the river.

ELODIE   All night I will!

ROSE   A moment, then, and I'll follow.

ELODIE touches her neck-cord

ELODIE   Look. We both wear these. Now we're always sisters.
                 Philippe!

ELODIE goes. ROSE watches her, then turns, walks back to the table and blows out the candle. She kneels, picks up the two books, and remains there, looking at them

Fade to darkness

www.ingramcontent.com/pod-product-compliance
Ingram Content Group UK Ltd.
Pitfield, Milton Keynes, MK11 3LW, UK
UKHW031251020325
455690UK00007B/94